The Legend of Zelda Skyward Sword HD:

The Complete Guide & Walkthrough with Tips &Tricks

Fledgling's Guide and Tips

This page contains data on the most proficient method to begin in The Legend of Zelda: Skyward Sword for the Wii and Skyward Sword HD for the Switch. Here you'll discover fundamental tips that apply to most Zelda games, just as explicit deceives you may not think about your first time playing Skyward Sword.

Despite the fact that The Legend of Zelda: Skyward Sword has been viewed by some as one of the more "hand-holdy" Zelda games throughout the entire existence of the establishment, that doesn't mean its instructional exercises advise you without question, all that you require to know. Considering that, here's a fast Skyward Sword novice's aide brimming with tips.

The Usual Zelda Tips

For one thing, we should begin with the fundamental all inclusive Zelda tips that the majority of you likely definitely know, however on the off chance that this is your first time with a Zelda game: Make sure to get pixies in void jugs so they can basically give you an additional life when you lose your entire being, break every one of the pots and cut all the grass when you get yourself low on assets, bomb all dubious looking dividers for covered up bits of hearts, etc.

Overhaul Your Wallet As Soon As You Can

One thing you'll ultimately adapt very almost immediately in Skyward Sword is that you can gather 300 Rupees decently fast, and when you hit that edge, any rupees you gather after that should be tossed into the junk since they don't get added to any kind of Rupee bank account. So make a venture from the beginning and get a greater wallet.

You can get a little wallet from Beedle's Shop at the sensible cost of 100 Rupees, yet the huge wallets that expansion your maximum rupees by a ton must be gotten by finishing Side Quests and turning in your appreciation gems to Batreaux. We'll get to him later.

Try not to Open Goddess Chests With a Full Pouch of Rupees

Except if you know precisely the thing you're getting from a Goddess Chest, as I don't have the foggiest idea, perhaps you're utilizing our nitty gritty Walkthrough, you don't need open Goddess Chests with a full pocket of rupees. Like I said, any rupees you get past what you can as of now convey are totally squandered, and large numbers of the prizes you'll discover in these Goddess Chests are significant silver and gold rupees that can net you upwards of 300 rupees on the double. When you open a Goddess Chest and guarantee its award, you can't open it once more, so try not to squander those chances to become more extravagant.

Get out and about After Every Dungeon

It very well may be enticing to simply bounce solidly into a recently opened opening in the sky to investigate the following district, however consistently make a point to get out and about through Skyloft, Pumpkin Landing, Bamboo Island, etc. Converse with local people, take on Side Quests, scrutinize the marketplace for new things, open Goddess Chests, et cetera. The prizes are quite often worth the additional work.

Money In Your Gratitude Crystals

Thusly, when you do finish a sidequest, recall that you need to turn in your Gratitude Crystals to Batreoux, who is a NPC that shows up after you complete the Lost Child sidequest. You can begin this mission just in the wake of finishing the primary significant prison and is set off by chatting with Wryna after you leave the yard in Skyloft.

You'll skip from Skyloft to the Lumpy Pumpkin and back again to find a secret passage in the cemetery that will take you to Batreoux's refuge. When you talk with him, each side journey you do after that will remunerate you with Gratitude Crystals that you can take back to him for an award, similar to bits of heart, bigger wallets, and then some.

Utilize Skyward Strikes in Combat

Upward Strikes aren't only for initiating extravagant components. They're additionally an entirely significant battle device and are an incredible method to start battles. They're amazing, can hit numerous objectives immediately, and are likewise an incredible way at managing things like bee colonies, crows, and different adversaries that attempt to assault from a good ways.

There's Generally More Than One Way To Kill an Enemy

An incredible aspect regarding Skyward Sword is that foes can be crushed in countless manners. You can basically assault the openings in a foe's gatekeeper, you could likewise sit tight for them to assault and hit them with a safeguard repel to stagger them, you could send your creepy crawly to cut the stem of a Deku Baba, you can take care of a bomb to one of the gold deku babas, you could wound their stem, you can daze an adversary with the slingshot, et cetera.

Point is, if any one strategy is giving you inconvenience, require one moment to take a gander at your stock and analysis to check whether whatever else gives you a simpler time.

Deal with What Shield You're Using

Until you get the best safeguard in the game, the indestructible Hylian Shield, you'll need to take care with respect to what safeguard you're utilizing against which foes. Clearly the Iron Shield is a preferred alternative over the wooden one much of the time, yet in case you're going toward electric adversaries, the steel safeguard will really accomplish more damage than anything else.

Try not to Attack Randomly

Adversaries in Skyward Sword are intentionally intended to have the option to impede arbitrary wild blade assaults, also that you're most likely going to wear yourself out. In case you're attempting to drive an opening in Bokoblin foes, you regularly can in the event that you swing left and solidly in a consistent musicality, however in case you're simply swinging your sword pretty much all higgledy piggledy, you will get hindered usually.

Catch Bugs

Bugs are wherever in Skyward Sword, and on the off chance that you get yourself a net from Beedle's shop in Skyloft, you can get them and transform them into an assortment of elixirs by visiting Bertie in the Bazaar. Recuperating elixirs specifically are incredibly significant, in light of the fact that while hearts aren't too difficult to find, they have a negative propensity of being no place in sight when you need them the most.

Switch Motion Control Tips

This page contains data on Skyward Sword HD for the Nintendo Switch's new movement control arrangement, and tips to take advantage of it.

At the point when previously delivered for the Nintendo Wii, Skyward Sword was totally worked around movement controls - which makes porting it to a control center that doesn't have a similar degree of movement regulator support sort of precarious. Yet, Nintendo appears to have sorted it out with Skyward Sword HD, making it completely playable with no kind of movement controls utilizing either the Switch Gamepad or a Pro Controller. How can it function? All things considered, how about we investigate and discover.

Tips for Camera Controls

One of the large new things that Skyward Sword HD adds according to a control viewpoint is the capacity to openly control the camera with the right stick, something in a real sense incomprehensible on the Wii due to there just being one control stick.

At the point when you're playing without movement controls however, things work somewhat diversely because of the way that the right stick is the place where Nintendo has set your sword controls.

So assuming you need to move the camera, you'll need to initially hold down the left guard and afterward move the stick. It takes some becoming acclimated to, yet luckily, there's likewise the choice of simply doing the exemplary 3D Zelda thing of focusing the camera behind Link with Z-focusing by squeezing the left trigger.

Tips for Sword Combat

Battle is the place where things see the greatest change, and's a few key things to make note of:

Leading is the way that, on the grounds that the game was initially planned around heading explicit assaults as opposed to the more conventional "simply cut anything that's before you," you need to flick the right stick toward the path you need to slice. Rapidly move the stick toward a path and afterward immediately let it get back to its ordinary position. It's a bit fussy, and takes some training to truly get the hang of - if the stick doesn't go right to the edge, you will not get a slice; if the stick hangs on the edge for a really long time, you will not get a slice. It simply needs a speedy flick.

The second significant thing that you need to know is that when you face a foe that squares toward a path, you need to really flick the stick toward the path that they are guarding. So if a Lizalfos is impeding to one side, you need to flick the adhere to one side, on the grounds that the stick movement copies the way of the blade. It's not "Hit the left side," it's really "swing the blade from the right to left." It's a bit irrational, yet fundamentally, rather than considering them safeguarding themselves, consider them holding up a sign that says "assault here." That said, it's anything but an ideal procedure. These folks appeared to hinder from down underneath even while they were obstructing high, so, all in all, I'd say simply utilize an even cut.

Cuts, or forward pushes, are taken care of by clicking in the right stick, while safeguard repels are taken care of by clicking in the left stick, Skyward Strikes should really be possible significantly more effectively by essentially holding the right stick up, lastly you can likewise utilize turn assaults by rapidly moving the stick left, right left; right, left, right; down, up, down; or up, down, up.

Other Motion Control Tips

Everything in Skyward Sword HD works essentially as you'd anticipate. Rather than holding up the distant and throwing bombs, for instance, you should simply prepare a bomb, move the right stick up, and press the right trigger. You can ride your bird with ordinary stick controls; the harp can be played simply by moving the right stick to and fro, and whatever would normally utilize movement controls to point, presently can utilize the Splatoon esque-mixture pointing situation that utilizes both the right stick and the Switch's gyro controls on the genius regulator or gamepad.

Walkthrough

The Wing Ceremony

Converse with Pipit, the understudy wearing a yellow tunic to study the Wing Ceremony. Then, at that point, head a few doors down and converse with Fledge, who is remaining by a couple huge barrels. He will request that you convey a barrel to the elderly person in the kitchen. Controls: You can check your guide by squeezing "+". Certain items, like pots and barrels, can be gotten and conveyed by remaining close to them and squeezing "A". To tenderly set an item on the ground, tap "A". To toss a conveyed object, point the Wii far off up and flick forward. To move an item, point the Wii distant down and flick up.

Endurance Meter: The Stamina Meter is a green circle that seems at whatever point Link is accomplishing something debilitating, for example, conveying a substantial article, running, utilizing a twist assault, and climbing. In the event that your endurance meter runs out totally you'll turn out to be briefly gasping for air, and will not be able to convey anything or utilize your gear until it re-energizes. At the point when your meter is practically vacant, you should quit playing out any debilitating activity and sit tight for it to top off.

Convey the barrel into the kitchen, watching out for your endurance meter. After you convey the barrel into the kitchen, return to Fledge and converse with him. He will remunerate you with a Red Rupee, worth 20 Rupees.

Leave the institute through the enormous swinging doors. Here you will track down your first of many Bird Statues, what work as the game's save focuses.

Bird Statues: Since there is no programmed saving in this game, Bird Statues are your solitary alternative for recording your advancement. They show up much of the time all through the game, so it's a smart thought to save at whatever point you experience one.

After you leave the foundation, a man will shout to you from over the entryway. His name is Instructor Horwell.

Controls: You can lock on to individuals, adversaries, and items by confronting them and squeezing and holding the "Z" trigger on the Nunchuk. While focusing on them, you can converse with companions from a distance by squeezing the "A" button.

Converse with Professor Horwell, and he'll advise you to run up the containers close by to arrive at the space where he's standing. Run towards the containers to scale on top of them, then, at that point hop across the short hole by running towards it.

Significant: This game doesn't highlight a "hop button". All things being equal, Link will hop consequently at whatever point you walk rapidly or run off of an edge.

Note that there's a discourse bubble above Professor Horwell. Discourse bubbles generally demonstrates an individual has something critical to say, relating to either the Main Quest, or a Side Quest.

Assuming you need to help Instructor Horwell discover Mia, you can by ascending the close by edge and shimmying around. Hop across a couple of holes and afterward move up the plants to the space over the Academy. Push the container against the divider on the arrival and move up and get the hairy animal.

Endurance Fruit: A green Stamina Fruit is on the ground here. at the point when you contact an endurance organic product, your endurance meter will be quickly topped off. This makes it simpler to move rapidly around Skyloft.

In the wake of managing Professor Horwell, head past the Bird Statue towards the steps before the Academy. From here, you can take one of two ways. One way drives you directly to Zelda where a cutscene will start while the other way is a diversion towards a chest that contains a Red (20) Rupee. Taking the way towards the chest is the most ideal choice since it will ultimately lead you to the cutscene with Zelda at any rate (and Rupees aren't in every case simple to stop by).

To go directly to the cutscene with Zelda, pass through the entryway. To take the way to the chest, look towards the right, from the close by endurance organic product, and there will be an earthy colored box where you can drop down to (try to glance around with the C catch to ensure you will not drop off the guide!). From on top of the earthy colored box, drop to the cold earth beneath and afterward drop down once more (you wont bring harm from simply dropping down). From that point, bounce across the hole and head straight down the way until it parts into two. Take the way on the right, it will lead you to the chest that contains 20 Rupees.

After you acquire the Rupees, head back up, to where the way parts into two, and take the way on the left. Run up the divider with the goal that you swing from the edge and shimmy your direction right across to the opposite side. Drop down and head down the way until you arrive at a precarious stone slope. Run up the stone slope to get to the top and afterward get around to the gliding island close by. It is at the highest point of the gliding island where you will initially see heart blossoms that will renew your wellbeing when you go through them to get them. From here, leap to the verdant divider and climb as far as possible up to the top. You are presently at where you meet Zelda and when you stroll forward a bit the cutscene will initiate.

As you talk with her you can pick what you need to say. Your decisions will not influence the game, just Zelda's reactions.

After the cutscene, Zelda will push you off the bluff. Press DOWN on the D-Pad to call your Loftwing. He will not show up!

After the cutscene, you need to discover Professor Horwell. Head back to the Academy, right down the means toward the southwest. (You can discover a clue about what befell your Loftwing by conversing with the man fixing the entryway at the lower part of the steps.

Additionally, conversing with Fledge inside the institute uncovers that he knows something about what befell your Loftwing.)

Just external the Academy (to one side of the entryway) is Professor Horwell. Presently, head to the stone Light Tower in the southern Plaza region. A kid will stop you en route to discuss bugs.

You can move into the tree utilizing the Nunchuk and a Sky Stag Beetle will show up (on the off chance that you roll into different trees around, they will drop blue (5) Rupees).Touch it to get it. Peruse up about bugs in the Bug Collection area.

In the Plaza you'll discover your adversaries in the present race, Groose, Cawlin and Strich. You will start a cutscene with exchange decisions when you approach them.

Obviously, your bird has been caught by these jerks. Individuals will advise you to discover Pipit now. He's at the Sparring Hall conversing with Fledge.

Head back to the Sparring Hall in the northwest and converse with Pipit. He'll show you Waterfall Cave on your guide. It's on the east side. Prior to going, you'll need a blade.

Enter the Sparring Hall. Converse with the huge person in front, then, at that point head through the entryway into the back. Here is a chest containing the Practice Sword.

You would now be able to converse with the person in front for a blade exercise in the event that you so want. Practice your slices on the logs in the room.

Controls: Basic slices are cultivated by essentially swing the Wii far off toward any path. You can push with your sword by making a wounding movement straight towards the screen. You can swing both nunchuk and Wii distant one way to do a twist assault, however know: utilizing turn assaults depletes a part of your endurance meter. You can play out the Fatal Blow on fallen foes. Essentially Shake both Wii Remote and Nunchuck simultaneously to hop up and wound the fallen foe.

Sheikah Stone: When you leave the Sparring Grounds, a Sheikah Stone will emerge starting from the earliest stage. It contains an assortment of video clues to help you on the off chance that you at any point stall out during the Main Quest, and will likewise incorporate some additional recordings for some Side Quest related exercises. More clue recordings will open as you progress through the game.

Presently, go directly toward Waterfall Cave, situated close to Skylofts just enormous waterway. Head towards where the water tumbles off the edge of Skyloft and bounce across the stages to arrive at the opposite side.

Keep strolling towards the cascade. You will discover a cavern entrance with a few wood posts before it. Chop down the posts with your sword and enter the cavern.

Cascade Cave

Slash down the posts with the blade. Inside the cavern are Keese. Cut fiercely to kill them. Chu Chus will jump onto you in the event that you draw near. Nail them with fundamental assaults to kill them. On the off chance that they hook one, waggle the Wii Remote as show to get free.

Finish the single way the cavern. In the event that you check the guide, you can see the way you are taking - zoom in to see the dabs in your way.

Finish the way the cavern until you see a fence on the right. Head to the messed up piece of the fence, toward the end, and leap to the edge that contains two heart blossoms and a chest that contains a Red (20) Rupee. Drop to the cold earth beneath and proceed down the cavern way.

Run to get up the lofty grade at the lower part of the inclining way. You can climb a few plants on the southern edge of the cavern to discover a Chest with a Red Rupee in it.

The genuine fortune is a reserve of two Red Rupees close to the exit. Chop down the grass by the exit and slither into the little opening to get them.

Leave the cavern and save at the Bird Statue. Zelda will go along with you.
You'll see the Crimson Loftwing ahead. Cut the four rope spots on each side of the blocked region to free the bird.

With your bird free you would now be able to travel to the service. After the cutscene, hop of the edge and press DOWN on the D-Pad. This time your Loftwing will get you.

The guidelines given are a bit misle

ading - to fly you'll need to accomplish more than slant here and there. The key is to swing your Wii far off upward to fold the bird's wings and gain elevation. The waving movement is to some degree like waving a goliath fan at the TV. After you acquire tallness, slant the Wii Remote down to plunge. This is the means by which you can dominate races and get around rapidly.

Squeezing the A catch will give you a scramble of speed, yet you have restricted runs (set apart as plumes on your screen) that will re-energize. Squeezing the B catch will back you off.

After the instructional exercise, Zelda will say that your Loftwing looks fine and that you both ought to go to her dad to reveal to him the uplifting news.

A screen inquiring as to whether you might want to save will spring up so ensure that you save. After you pick if to save, you and Zelda will be back on the ground and have a little discussion until she passes on to disclose to her dad that your Loftwing is okay. Groose will then, at that point appear with Cawlin and Strich. It will ultimately be obvious that he is charmed by Zelda. Zelda will then, at that point appear behind Groose separating his little fantasy about him and her alone. He then, at that point leaves with his partners in crime and Zelda wishes you best of luck in your race.

A declaration for every one of the understudies to collect for the race is then made and a cutscene will start.

The Race

To begin the race, you should run out to the board walkway and bounce off the edge. Call your Loftwing by pushing Down on the D-Pad and the race will formally begin. The objective of the race is to get the yellow bird with the little sculpture. Take a gander at your rise meter.

Gradually fold your wings by going here and there with the Wii Remote and when you get to the top, run down. Utilize the A Button run to traverse the last distance among you and the bird. Just at the highest point of the rise meter should you jump down. This requires unobtrusive developments, not wild moving.

After you get the bird once, Groose and his associates will toss eggs at you to keep you from getting the little sculpture. You then, at that point should get the bird a subsequent time.

This time, notwithstanding, you should avoid shots, however making up for lost time to the bird requires similar climbing and plunging standards.

After the race, a cutscene will initiate and you will be granted with the Sailcloth.

You will then, at that point need to test it out, after the long cutscene with Zelda, via arriving in the circle beneath.

Move the Wii far off around to direct your fair and not long before you hit the ground, hit the B catch to pull out your Sailcloth to land securely.

After you land securely, another cutscene will play and Fi will get in touch with you during it.

At the point when you awaken, Zelda is gone and you are back in the Knight Academy. After the cutscene with Gaepora, you acquire control once more. You can open the bureau for a Blue Rupee once more. Out in the corridor the spooky figure of Fi will show up. Follow her up the steps and down the corridor and afterward outside. The door to the Goddess Statue is locked, and Fi will lead you down certain edges toward its east.

The freaky feline you experience can be discarded without any problem. Cut it a couple of times and it will grovel in dread. You can, be that as it may, get it and lose it the bluff, in case you are an awful individual. (Try not to feel really awful however, given a second the monster will fold back up utilizing it's ears.)

Drop of the edge to one side and open the Chest for a Red Rupee (on the off chance that you got the chest before you get together with Zelda at the Goddess Statue, then, at that point you will not need to stress over getting the chest).

You can bounce up and get the edge Fi drives you to. Move passed on to crawl along the edge.

Run up the slope, killing any Keese or Chu Chus in your manner. Leap to the plants and climb them, shaking the Wii Remote to run upwards.

At the point when you get to the top, keep on pursuing Fi around the sculpture until a cutscene will begin showing Fi vanish inside the sculpture.

After she vanishes, a passageway will show up, at the spot she vanished at, which is your sign to head inside the sculpture.

Inside the Statue of the Goddess

Inside the sculpture is a way to a room with a sword on a platform. Stroll towards the room and a cutscene will begin. Fi reveals to you that she is the soul of the sword and it is her obligation to serve you in your fate. She will likewise advise you that Zelda is alive and to save her you should take the sword.

Approach the blade and press the A catch to analyze it. Utilize the Wii Remote, by adhering to the directions on screen, to yank the blade out.

After the blade is out, hold the Wii distant up to the sky and hold it there while a beam of light radiates down the sword. You have now procured the Goddess Sword.

Another cutscene will begin where Gaepora will discover you in the sculpture and you will get the Emerald Tablet, one of three tablets that total a board.

Approach the peak and utilize a Skyward Strike on the blue wing insignia (hold the Wii Remote pointing upwards, then, at that point swipe the sharp edge once it is completely energized). After you do as such, place the tablet in the board.

Another cutscene will begin in which a little break opens in the cloud boundary permitting you to arrive at the surface. You would now be able to converse with Fi utilizing DOWN on the D-Pad any time you wish. Gaepora will then, at that point reveal to you that you will require a more tough outfit and that your uniform for dominating the race should now be prepared for you.

A screen will spring up inquiring as to whether you need to save so pick if to save.

After you do as such, a short cutscene will begin showing you putting on the Green Uniform. Superintendent Gaepora will then, at that point urge you to visit the Bazaar prior to leaving Skyloft.

At the point when you leave the room, Fledge will call your name and approach you. He will then, at that point give you the Adventure Pouch which will permit you to store four things in it.

You can fill your Adventure Pouch with things from the Bazaar. The Adventure pocket can be extended each space in turn all through the game. You will not store principle things in this, similar to the Beetle or Slingshot, however consumable things and packaged things are put away here.

Head outside the Academy from the base floor and converse with Instructor Horwell simply off to one side. He will give you a free Wooden Shield. To prepare the safeguard, or some other thing, hold the - Button and spot the cursor over the thing you need to choose. Delivery the - catch to prepare it. Educator Horwell then, at that point proposes you to go to the Sparring Hall and figure out how to utilize a safeguard appropriately (this isn't obligatory to do, so assuming you like to sort out some way to get things done without anyone else, simply go directly toward the Bazaar).

Head over to the Sparring Hall and converse with the Instructor to figure out how to utilize a safeguard and how to do a safeguard slam. You can fix (or supplant) safeguards at the Bazaar in Skyloft. At the point when you pass through the door to get to the Bazaar, Fi will stop you and give you an idea to get a few elixirs (she will likewise advise you to purchase a safeguard however you will not require it since Instructor Horwell gives you a free safeguard) from the Bazaar. She will likewise educate you on the best way to change your on-screen show. To change your on-screen show, you need to press the 1 catch on the Wii distant.

Here are the depictions of the on-screen shows you can browse:

Interface Options

Standard - A Wii far off diagram on the right and catch design.

Light - Just fastens on the right.
Pro - Nothing yet hearts and Rupees.

After you get everything arranged the manner in which you need, head over to the Bazaar. It is simply toward the south of the Academy in the focal point of Skyloft (up the steps). In the Bazaar, you can do and purchase different things. There is a person in the Bazaar that will fix your safeguard and update your stuff for you. To update your stuff, you will require certain things that beasts drop, after you rout them, and a specific measure of Rupees.

There is additionally a woman that does an Item Check for you. Going to her permits you to put stuff in/take stuff out your Adventure Pouch from/into capacity. You can likewise sell certain replaceable things like safeguards and sacks.

A freaky man will disclose to you your fortune for 10 Rupees.

Notwithstanding, since it will be your first time having your fortune told, or the way that he hasn't had any clients in some time, he will just charge you 1 Rupee. So why not do it the first run through? All things considered, it is just 1 Rupee right?

 may, you can't accepting Bombs, Arrows or Seeds until you have a Slingshot, Bow or Bomb Bag.

Presently, on to the primary concern you came here to purchase, Potions. Converse with the mixture woman to get your first Empty Bottle!

At the Potion Shop you can purchase various kinds of elixirs. In any case, the lone mixtures you will actually want to purchase right now are the Heart Potion (worth 20 Rupees; renews eight hearts), Revitalizing Potion (worth 30 Rupees; fixes broken safeguards and reestablishes four hearts), or the Guardian Potion (worth 200 Rupees; parts the measure of harm you take for some time). The decision is yours on which mixture to purchase.

Converse with the man close to the mixture shop, blending at the cauldron, to "mix" elixirs with bugs from your assortment. Notwithstanding, you can't do that until you have purchased a Bug Net from Beedle's Shop.

Note that there is a blue Chest in the Bazaar you can't open. This can be opened exclusively by discovering a Goddess Cube on The Surface underneath the mists. There are a greater amount of these around Skyloft, and you can't do anything about them now. You call down Beedle's Shop by tossing a pot or one more article at the chime, yet it's fairly troublesome, so it's ideal to leave the Bazaar and Skyloft.

At the point when you are all set through the break, do a running scramble off any wooden edge of the city and call your Loftwing by pushing Down on the D-Pad. You'll see an enormous, green section of light coming from the mists. Go to the green light and when you get close to it a cutscene will start.

Fixed Grounds

You will initially show up tumbling down to the land. Try to squeeze B to land securely. (Note that while falling get-togethers load screen, you will [sometimes] consequently utilize your Sailcloth. Some other type of falling won't utilize your Sailcloth consequently!) When you land securely, Fi will come show up before you and reveal to you that you are in the Sealed Grounds and to tread carefully.

Begin heading down the way, and you will experience Deku Babas interestingly. They are harder than in past Zelda games, and strong in the event that you don't swing your sword on the money - even or vertical relying upon how the mouth is open.

After you rout both of the Deku Babas, continue to run along the way until you run into two additional Deku Babas. Rout them rapidly and drop to the cold earth beneath for a cutscene to happen.

After the cutscene, continue forward (see that there is a locked entryway that you can't pass through yet off to one side) and you will see that the way parts into two. Take the way on the left since there is not all that much on the off chance that you take the other way.

You can likewise hop off the precipice to get to the base speedier. It's ideal in the event that you do the last since it will not take as long and there isn't anything to do when simply running down the way (except if you like cutting grass with your blade not getting a single thing from doing as such). On the off chance that you hop off the bluff, make a point to utilize the Sailcloth to securely land.

At the base, you will see a little platform delivering a dim air around it. Draw near enough to it and a voice will address you advising you to raise your sword up and strike the platform.

Raise your blade to energize it and afterward slice at the little platform with the Skyward Strike. After you do as such, steam spouts will show up nearby.

Fi will currently educate you concerning Dowsing. Dowsing permit you to detect a close by objective by checking out the space in First Person see. Press and hold C to actuate the Dowsing menu.

In this first-individual mode, a purple ring will highlight the article you are looking for. Your Wii distant will vibrate and you will hear a pinging clamor. The vibration becomes more prominent and the pinging clamor will get stronger as you look more toward your goal. Additionally, a purple bolt will show up on the ring when you are glancing in the right area. Lastly, the nearer you get, the greater the purple circle will become, and the pinging will heighten.

Pick the Zelda symbol from the Dowsing menu and check out the space until you see the bolt spring up on the ring. Follow the bolt to get to your objective. The steam rambles in this space can be utilized to fly upwards. Simply stroll over them and your Sailcloth will lift you up.

Follow the bolt from the Dowsing capacity, and it will carry you to the fixed entryway that was referenced before. Stroll over to the entryway and the token on the entryway can vanish permitting you to at long last enter through the entryway.

When you pass through the entryway, you will be in a sanctuary region. Inside this sanctuary is a Bird Statue, off to one side, so make a point to save your game at it. Off to the right is an entryway, yet you can't go through it at this time. All things being equal, look to one side, from the entryway, and you will recognize a Chest with a Revitalizing Potion inside it. Assuming you brought a Heart Potion prior to leaving the Bazaar at Skyloft, you will currently have two void jugs that you can utilize on the off chance that you utilize the elixirs.

Side Note: If you have both a Heart Potion and the Revitalizing Potion from the chest, then, at that point you should utilize the Heart Potion (regardless of whether it is for reasons unknown). The justification this is on the grounds that on the contrary side of the steps, close to the chest, one of the pots contains a Fairy in it that you can get in a vacant jug. Getting a Fairy will renew six hearts, like the Heart Potion, which recharges eight (yet you just have six hearts right now at any rate.) The just, and all that is required, distinction is that in the event that you have the Fairy and run out of hearts, the Fairy will naturally restore you back to life. Goodness, and in the event that you coincidentally miss the pixie with your container and it recuperates you unexpectedly, simply leave the sanctuary and return to bottle it (this additionally implies you can get a pixie here anytime in the game for the time being on).

Head up the steps and you will experience a puzzling old woman who will disclose to you that she has been hanging tight numerous years for your appearance and will likewise reveal to you that Zelda has made a beeline for Faron Woods. She will then, at that point mark the area of Faron Woods on your guide for you and advise you to put a signal on the red X.

To put the guide, open your guide and move the pointer over the red X. Press the C catch to put the guide on it. You go through the C catch to pick and drop the reference point. Try to zoom in on the off chance that you truly need to be exact when putting reference points.

Save your game, assuming you need, and leave through the eastern entryway that the old woman opens for you. At the point when you stroll outside, you will see the light emission beaming down where you put your guide at.

Head down the way and you will experience Bokoblins irritating a Goron. Head toward them and battle the Bokoblins to save the Goron. Bokoblins protect in the position you move your sword to, so make a point to assault the second they let their gatekeeper down to assault you. You can likewise utilize a Shield Bash to make them drop their defenses (time it for when the Bokoblin assaults); yet remember that utilizing your Shield without utilizing a Shield Bash will make it lose solidness with each hit.

After you rout the Bokoblins, you will converse with the Goron. His name isGorko, and he will inform you concerning the historical backdrop of the Bird Statue. After he is finished talking, the Bird Statue he is remaining close to will start to gleam when you approach it. Here you can save, however head out back to the sky!

Move up the plants that are close by and enter through the opening in the divider. At the point when you go through it, it will return you to the start of the Sealed Grounds. Push the sign before you to make a speedy alternate route from behind the Temple back to the Sealed Grounds. Head back through the opening in the divider and pass through the open entryway by Gorko and the Bird Statue. Push the log close by to the precipice divider and move up to continue down the way.

Faron Woods

A cutscene will initiate and Fi will come out revealing to you that Zelda is without a doubt nearby and to continue utilizing your Dowsing capacity to look for her. Save at the Bird Statue and afterward run towards the rope to take hold of it to swing across the hole.

It's ideal on the off chance that you slice down the grass to uncover brambles. Brambles are spikey balls that append on to you and explode to harm you. On the off chance that a bramble appends to you, do a Sword Spin to shake it off before it explodes.

Proceed down the way and you will experience some more Bokoblins that are presently annoying a Kikwi. Rout the Bokoblins and afterward converse with the Kikwi. He will botch you as a Bokoblin and flee in dread.

Fi will then, at that point show up and reveal to you that the Kikwi has an energy spike that is near Zelda's and recommend that you follow it to discover why it does.

Follow the Kikwi by running up the slope and proceed down the way until a cutscene will happen showing the Kikwi fleeing some more. After the cutscene is done, glance over to one side and save at the Bird Statue. After you save, head down the way to the rollable log (you will realize what direction is the right way in light of the fact that Fi will come out revealing to you that you should continue to scan the region for the Kikwi everytime you head off course) and roll it down the bluff to make an alternate way to the passageway of the forest.

Make a point to likewise get the Amber Relic collectible close to where the log was at previously. After you do as such, utilize your Dowsing capacity to follow precisely where the Kikwi is at.The Kikwi will take cover behind various mushrooms nearby. At the point when you discover the mushroom that it is behind, cut at the mushroom to make it emerge from covering up. At the point when it withdraws behind a tree, it will stop. Machi presents itself and reveals to you Zelda is secluded from everything with the Elder Kikwi.

Side N Make sure to see that there is a Bomb-capable Wallon the eastern side of this space. In any case, you will require bombs to bomb it and to get bombs you need a Bomb Bag. When you get the Bomb Bag and a few bombs, return here and bomb the divider to get the Heart Piece that is behind it.

Fi will come out and mark Machi on your guide for you. She will then, at that point disclose to you that the Elder will without a doubt have similar Dowsing readings as Zelda, as Machi did, and to continue utilizing your Dowsing capacity to discover them.

Head southeast dependent on the Dowsing signal. There's a Bird Statue here. Run up the incline past the Deku Baba plant.

To kill it, get a rock at the top and throw it down at the plant. Climb the cascade/edge in the pool in the southeast corner and you can get another Amber Relic.

In this next region is an Oktorok (Grass). These plants jump out of the ground when you are far away to nail you with nuts. These nuts WILL harm your safeguard, so be careful!

On the off chance that your safeguard becomes harmed, you'll need to go fix a safeguard in Skyloft at the Scrap Shop or utilize a Revitalizing Potion. Observe that safeguards which get totally annihilated, must be supplanted, they can't be fixed! You can quick head out back to any purple Bird Statue you've recently saved immediately you get back on your bird. In this way, it's ideal to disregard these Oktoroks for the time being. To kill them nonetheless, use nunchuk pokes (the Shield Bash procedure) to send the shots back at the right second. On the off chance that appropriately planned, a Shield Bash forestalls harm to your safeguard while likewise counter-assaulting your adversary.

Run due south and you can run up a bended incline past a Bird Statue to a rope. Cut the rope and it will end up being a rope swing. Use it to arrive at the focal point of the space.

The Kikwi Elder is snoozing here. You can go around him for the time being and drop off the western edge of his foundation to get another Amber Relic. These can be utilized to update your Wooden Shield. Push the log off the precipice here also to make an alternate way and uncover another Amber Relic.

Kikwi Hunt

Bucha, the Kikwi Tribe Elder, is feeling the loss of some Kikwis. To get more data on the whereabouts of Zelda, you should assist with discovering them utilizing the Dowsing capacity.

Kikwi Locations Map

Kikwi 1: Lopsa

Simply past the senior, on his foundation is a little opening. Slither through it to a cave inside the immense tree. Here you can gather up a Fairy in your jug (you'll need to exhaust a jug, prepare it, LOCK ON to the pixie and press A to swipe the jug and catch it). Climb the plants here to arrive at another space.

Here is a rope you can move across. Hold the Wii Remote up in an upward direction to adjust in transit across. Slant it to address your walk. While hanging, you can Jostle the rope by shaking the Wii Remote. This will shake the pods off of the rope.

Approach the Bokoblin on the opposite side and a snare will happen. You can load up on hearts during the fight on the edges of the space. Use turn assaults to assault numerous Bokoblins on the double (and remember you can do vertical twist assaults as well).

Assault them with level cuts when their weapons are held evenly, and assault them with vertical cuts when their weapons are held upward. You can likewise endeavor Shield Bashes, yet be careful with harm to your safeguard in the event that you don't time them accurately!

On the off chance that you land a twist assault on one, it will wreck it and permit you to utilize a Fatal Blow.The Kikwi is up in the tree here. Roll into the tree to cut Lopsa down.

Utilize the plant to swing out of the space. Push down the log to make a way back.

The sanctuary with the incredible vantage point is your next objective.

Kikwi 2: Erla

There is a little structure with a decent vantage point on top in the west and from here you can get a reasonable perspective on the Kikwi. Climb the sanctuary steps and, by the Bird Statue, look or dowse for the closest Kikwi.

The one in the upper east is on an edge that has a few plants on the divider paving the way to it. Imprint it on your guide. You can climb those plants and utilize the Leap movement to arrive at the Kikwi.

There is a Bombable Wall here you can return for some other time, it conceals a chest with a Goddess Plume in it.

To wake the Kikwi, clear all the grass. Erla is represented, so there is one more to go.

Kikwi 3: Oolo

Slither back through the little opening south of the sanctuary. In the west is a slope/tree root that paves the way to a little red block facade and an opening in the ground (this is simply over the Sealed Grounds exit).

Drop through the opening and follow the way to the Kikwi, Oolo.

Heart Piece

The focal tree in the northern bit of Faron Woods has many roots. One root driving up from the south prompts a rope that you can swear on to this current Mother's grave Piece.

After you track down all the Kikwis, and acquire the Heart Piece, return back to Bucha and converse with him. He will thank you by disclosing to you where Zelda went to and give you a prize too.

From the Kikwi's back springs the Slingshot! You can utilize this to fire Deku Seeds.

A little, twisted plant is over the Elder Kikwi. You can shoot this twist to cut down a plant. Sweet!

(Note: If you shoot this from his back subsequent to getting the slingshot, or even roll into the tree prior to getting the slingshot, you can see some substitute discourse!)

Behind the structure with the incredible vantage point in the far north is an edge with another twisted plant above it. Destroy the plant and swing into the following region.

Make sure to move into trees and cut down plants for Deku Seeds in the event that you need ammunition for your Slingshot.

Profound Woods

Rout the Bokoblins in this first region. You can destroy the hornets' home or roll into the tree toward the west to cut down the hive. You might get some Hornet Larvae for your fortune assortment!

In the event that the hornets pursue you, flee from the hive area. They will before long disseminate.

Dowsing will lead you toward the north. In the following region is a rope connect. You can cross it, yet first you should kill the hive above it with the Slingshot. The hornets will drop into the pit beneath, alongside their hive.

Cross the rope and move up on the left of the way to push a log off an edge and make an alternate way.

Gorko will return now needing assistance. Continue to go downhill and you can jump onto an edge. This takes you to another rope way. On this way, shake off the brambles AND the Bokoblin when it gets close to you by waving the Wii distant while hanging.

Save at the Bird Statue at the highest point of the slope. Presently, cautiously run out to the rope. Swing a couple of times to get the force to arrive at the far side. You need to painstakingly swing, with to and fro movements of the Wii Remote.

It is here that you will initially experience a yellow Deku Baba named a Quadro-Baba. These dislike customary Deku Baba since they can take a LOT of hits and change the situation of its mouth. Watch for freedoms to cut it to overcome it. Try to snatch the money box close by (which contains a Red (20) Rupee is in it). Get together with Gorko, who has discovered a Goddess Cube. These shapes open money boxes in the sky. They will be set apart on your guide by Fi when you get back to the sky so you can track down the opened chests without any problem. Here are for the most part the Goddess Cube and chest areas, and what's inside too:

Goddess Cube

Utilize the Skyward Strike to open the Goddess Cube and it will vanish. Another Goddess Cube is directly down the steps here. They open chests with a Heart Piece and an Adventure Pouch Expansion.

You might need to get back to the sky since you have the Slingshot. You can call down Beedle's Shop in Skyloft and gather your Goddess Cube fortune for sure.

Beedle's Shop

Converse with the close by Bird Statue to get back to the sky. Fly to Skyloft and land close to the Bazaar. Point a Slingshot pellet up at Beedle's boat, which ought to be close to the Bazaar. Hit the ringer and he'll drop a rope. Snatch the rope and you will be pulled up to the shop.

The shop has costly costs, however for the time being you can buy the Bug Net (which is just 50 Rupees).

This is what you can purchase from Beedle:

Bug Net - 50 Rupees (Catch bugs for the Bug Collection)

Extra Wallet - 100 Rupees (Carry 300 extra Rupees)

Life Medal - 800 Rupees (Adds a Heart Container on the off chance that you have it in your Adventure Pouch)

Adventure Pouch Upgrade - 300 Rupees (Increases Adventure Pouch openings by 1)

Purchase a Bug Net and an Extra Wallet if possible. Fix your safeguard

assuming it needs it and, head back to the Forest Temple Bird Statue.
Skyview Temple

The huge entryway of Skyview Temple is locked, however a shot from your Slingshot will open it. Shoot the blue pearl at the highest point of the way to get a blue rupee (5). Search for a pink precious stone over the entryway. Shoot it and you will access the Skyview Temple.

At the point when you get inside, Fi will educate you that you can not follow Zelda with the Dowsing capacity any longer. Save at the Bird Statue before you and observe that the Go to the Sky choice is presently supplanted with Go Outside.

After you save, run down the twisting way and cut the trees and networks from a good ways (don't get trapped in the networks or you'll be defenseless to Keese assaults). On the off chance that you slice through the sparkling piece of tree stalks you'll get a Rupee reward. You will ultimately get to a high edge with grass on it to ascend it (just as a locked entryway to one side).

Chop down the trees before the edge. Before you climb, shoot the Deku Baba up top the edge with your slingshot to daze it. Move up the edge, rout the Deku Baba, and strike the pink precious stone to open the entryway.

In the new room, there's an Eye Switch. Lock on to it and point your blade at it. Do huge roundabout movements with the blade in a clockwise way while pointing directly at the TV. The Eye Switch will follow your developments; moving its eye toward the path you move the blade.

The Eye will ultimately become red and tumble off causing the entryway beneath it will open.

Enter through the entryway and you will see a few Burs spread around the space. You will likewise experience two Deku Babas that will dangle from the roof. Rout the adversaries and save at the Bird Statue. There are four entryways in this room on each side.

Continue forward on the scaffold and you will see a Green Gokoblin. This specific Bokoblin has a hatchet so you'll have to keep an eye out for its assaults. After you rout it, shoot the pink switch over the way to one side, however don't enter it yet.

Drop down beneath and scan the ground for some extra Rupees. A pink switch is very much covered up under the scaffold on the left side.

You can nail it with a Slingshot pellet or run up the edge it's on to hit it with your sword. Hitting this switch will open the entryway on the left side.

Head through the entryway on the left side and kill the Green Bokoblin in this room. You will see a Skulltula on a web here. You can not overcome it from the side you are on, so shoot the plant twists off to one side to sidestep the creepy crawlies. Swing across the plants to the far side and you will experience a Quadro-Baba.

Rout it and you can now you can wound the Skulltulas on the web. To do as such, either cut its stomach in the sparkling spot by doing a push with your blade (poking with the Wii Remote) or shoot them with the Slingshot and utilize Fatal Blows on them.

Tip: If you experience a Skulltula on the ground, a vertical slice (an upward cut from the base up) or, far superior, a vertical twist assault, will thump them on their back and furthermore consider a Fatal Blow.

After you rout the Skulltulas on the stone scaffold, glance around and you will see a pink switch here that can be shot with the Slingshot. Hitting this switch occupies the focal room up with water.

Run out through the entryway on the opposite side of the extension, inverse from where you entered, and you will have returned to the fundamental chamber that is currently overflowed with water.

From here, move up the tree limb, on the left, and you will discover a chest that contains the Dungeon Map.

The guide will show the area of Zelda and all the money boxes in the prison (No more compass!).

It will likewise show you the areas of all locked entryways, save focuses, and switches (the red X's) in the prison.

Presently, drop down to the extension in the primary chamber and head through the other entryway on the right. There is a little passage at the lower part of this space to one side. Drop down and creep through it to track down a pink switch over the enormous sculpture.

Hit the switch with a shot from your trusty Slingshot and the sanctuary will be loaded up with more water. At the point when the sanctuary wraps topping off with more water, climb the plants in the space to get out. You will see a Dig Spot here that you will get back to later.

Head back to the fundamental chamber and utilize the coasting sign on the right side, close to the entryway you passed through a couple of seconds prior, to get onto the plants (try to overcome the child Skulltula on the plant before you move up it!).

Climb the plants and pass through the entryway up here to return to the room you were only beforehand in.

Kill the Skulltula discovered dangling from the roof by cutting it evenly with your blade to turn it on its web.

At the point when the purple flimsy part on its back is uncovered, pushed your sword forward to harm it. After you kill it, turn and take a gander at the pair of Eye Switches that are keeping a chest in a correctional facility.

Remain before the two of them on the light fix (ensure that both of the eyes are taking a gander at you).

Pull out your blade and entrance the eyes, very much like last time, with wide roundabout movements. The eyes will ultimately tumble off and the bars limiting the chest will disappear.

In the chest is a Small Key for the Northern room in the principle chamber. Head back to the principle chamber and utilize the key on the locked northern entryway.

At the point when you go into the room, you will see the transcending stone design before you.

Confronting you is a locked entryway which can be opened by shotting the pink switch found simply above it. Prior to entering, ensure you are prepared to battle the small scale supervisor inside!

Stalfos

The Stalfos holds its blades in different points. To harm it, you need to situate your blade's swings with the goal that they strike its body in the space between the swords. (Ex: If it holds it's swords evenly, swipe on a level plane so your blade hits its ribcage in the space between them, as presented beneath.) Its rib confine will fall away as you assault. Continue to swipe from oppurtunistic points and you will take it out.

Inside the chest here is the Beetle. The Beetle can be utilized to recover things, cut cobwebs, explode bombs and actuate switches. You fire it and afterward control it distantly while it keeps going - getting things expands its reach.

Shoot the Beetle out through the opening in the divider and crush it straight into the pink gem that initially opened the entryway.

Back external the focal room, save at the Bird Statue and utilize the Beetle to investigate the region. Here's every one of the things you can kill and plunder you can get in the room:

You can chop down 3 boxes swinging from strings of web nearby to get a red rupees. One has a Pink Fairy in it. Catch it with your jug

Cut down the Skulltulas and afterward utilize a Finishing Blow to kill them.

Fly up into the entries over the locked entryway to discover rupees.

Fly up north over the banished entryway for a some blue rupees.

Fly up into an impasse in the south for a Red Rupee.

Above the locked entryway is a Red Rupee.

Fly up into the entry over the Bird Statue to hit a change to open the west entryway.

Heart Piece

An opening at the actual top of the focal design on the north side prompts a switch.

Send the Beetle up to this and hit it. This switch opens the door on the north side of the focal design with a Heart Piece inside!

Subsequent to utilizing your Beetle to hit the pink switch in the passage over the bird sculpture, enter the western entryway. Head straight down the foyer and enter the entryway toward the end. In this room, kill the Skulltula and you'll confront a triplet of Eye Switches.

Look behind you and send the Beetle up to chop down the crate hanging over the subsequent level. Move up there, by utilizing the lush divider, and push the crate down. Move it to the focal point of the room, with the goal that every one of the eyes will take a gander at you, and get on top.

At the point when you are up top the container and in the right position, every one of the three Eye Switches eyes will watch you. Hypnotize them with your sword in round movements and the door will open.

Open the chest, that was behind the entryway, and you will get another Small Key. You would now be able to open the eastern entryway in the room with the monstrous container. Leave the room and point the Beetle up at the wrecked step case.

Guide the Beetle to the pink switch, past the Skulltula on the web, and it will make more water ascend in the sanctuary. You would now be able to arrive at the messed up steps. Cut the Skulltula out of the web and kill it.

Head out the room, returning to the room with the gigantic jug, you go toward the Eastern entryway that is locked.

At the point when you approach the rope to stroll across, a few Deku Babas will hang down from the roof. Utilize your Beetle, focusing on their stem, to chop them down so you can securely cross the rope.

In the following entry, there is a three-headed beast called a Staldra which you can just kill by removing each of the three of its heads in a single swipe. Line up your swing right when the eyes become red and slice each head to kill it.
The simplest method to overcome it is to utilize your Wooden Shield to paralyze it, in the event that you time your Shield Bash, for right when the Staldra assaults.

At the point when you kill the Staldra another entryway will open up for you. Head through the recently opened entryway and you will be in another room with a Skulltula dangling from a strand. Utilize the Beetle to slice the strand making Skulltula tumble down into the pit.

Run bounce across the hole and you will see a door here that has a pink switch above it. Hit the switch with the bug to make an alternate way back to the room with the gigantic jug in it.

Cross the focal rope that leads towards the Boss Door. Two Green Gokoblins with come towards you from the front and behind. Jar the foes off the rope when they draw near to you.

A substitute technique is to bait the two Gokoblins onto the rope by getting on it yourself, and afterward get off and hit them with your slingshot.

They will be shocked and fall. At the point when you cross to the opposite side, make a point to save your game at the Bird Statue.

Turn left at the Boss Door for a red rupee in a Chest in a small room. Cross to the opposite side, of the Boss Door, to another little room and climb the plants.

Chop down a rope here and run leap to it. Swing towards the tree stage and climb the plants on it. Cautiously stroll along the tree and search for two twisted plants on the roof that you can hit with the Slingshot.

At the point when you hit the twisted plants, leap to the main plant. Line yourself up with the other plant by squeezing B and turning until you line up impeccably with it. Hurry to the lower part of the plant, swing, and leap to the following plant.

Swing to and fro on this plant until you have enormous force and you can take the leap into the little room.

Open the chest and you will get the Golden Carving (the 'Manager Key'). Move up the plants and leap out the little room. Get back over the rope and save at the Bird Statue by the supervisor entryway in the north. In the event that you don't have two recuperation things, and a safeguard, don't endeavor this supervisor battle! Get back to Skyloft to plan in case need be.

Go to the supervisor entryway and organize the Golden Carving to seem as though a lower-case 'h.'

You can utilize two hands to do this. Addition the Golden Carving when you have it arranged.

Chief: Ghirahim

In the event that you assault Ghirahim in a direct way, he will grab your blade. You should battle to break it liberated from his grip; in the event that you fall flat, Ghirahim will take your blade and use it against you. Utilize a Shield Bash to take it out of his hand, and afterward get it before he does. At the point when Ghirahim approaches you with his hand raised, he is observing your activities and moving his hand a similar way as your sword.

To ensure he doesn't get it, hang tight for him to hold his hand up and come exceptionally close, and draw it to any course of your decision. Then, at that point gradually (yet not very leisurely) move your sword to the OTHER heading and afterward cut at him a bundle, beginning with the bearing inverse his hand.

On the off chance that you move your sword to the opposite side excessively fast, the Wii Remote will decipher it as a slice, so watch out!

Tip: If you're truly experiencing difficulty, a methodology to rapidly complete the primary portion of the fight is to Skyward Strike him as he attempts to take your sword from you, then, at that point cut away at him before he can respond. On the off chance that you attempt to Skyward Strike him when he's distant, he'll move away, practically like he's transporting. You need to try not to Skyward Strike until he's impersonating your developments and attempting to take your blade.

Another tip is to protect slam (punch forward your nunchuk when safeguard is out) when he is close to you, then, at that point cut at him rapidly - I had a 90% achievement pace of this falling off while doing it and beat the initial segment of the fight rapidly.

Try not to freeze for the initial segment of the fight; he gives you heaps of time and you can simply continue to swing at him (with the expectation that a few slices will harm him), as long as you make sure to shake your distant determinedly when he snatches your blade. That way, he can't at any point truly get an assault on you, yet it's a patient fight.

In the wake of hitting him a bit, he will change strategies and fire some little shots at you. These can be smacked back at him with an ideal cut in the example of the shots. For example, in case they are in an upward line, slice in an upward line.

You'll need to move in an opposite direction from him while he lines up this assault. It is simpler to repulse the shots utilizing a Skyward Strike than an ordinary cut, yet it actually must be in the right point.

He will likewise do a scramble assault. Hold your safeguard out and utilize the nunchuk punch to repel Ghirahim when he runs into you. Then, at that point, swipe at him a bit. In the event that you lose your safeguard, in any case, you'll need to utilize a Spin Attack or ordinary swipes to hit him.

In the case of utilizing normal swipes, you should make a point to plan to either your right or left, whichever side he is assaulting, or you'll miss.

Infrequently Ghirahim will twist in near you with his sword raised. At the point when he does this, on a level plane cut at him.

Skyview Spring

After he takes a few dozen cuts, Ghirahim will withdraw. You will get a Heart Container that broadens your life for all time. Enter the entryway to get to the Skyview Spring.

Goddess Cube

Behind the spring by the cascades you can load up on a Pink Fairy or two.

Likewise, make certain to initiate the Goddess Cube (this opens a chest with a Gold Rupee on Pumpkin Landing) behind the place of worship with a Skyward Strike.

Presently, utilize the Skyward Strike to hit the blue wing image on the hallowed place itself.

Fi will decipher a message from the Gods for you and advise you that Zelda has cleansed herself at Skyview Spring. She will likewise disclose to you that she has without a doubt gone to Eldin Spring to satisfy her prediction. You'll then, at that point get the Ruby Tablet, which fits in the foundation of the enormous sculpture in Skyloft. Fi will advise you to get back to a Bird Statue and take it to Skyloft.

After you are done conversing with Fi, a cutscene will initiate showing Machi meeting you before the sanctuary, saying thanks to you for discovering the entirety of his companions, and wishing you karma on discovering Zelda. After the cutscene is done, save at the Bird Statue and go to the Sky.

The Goddess Cubes you've discovered now show up on your guide, situated on different islands in the Sky. Fi will disclose to you about this. This present time is as great an opportunity as any to snatch the substance of these chests. For the three you've found in Faron Woods up to this point you'll get a Heart Piece, Adventure Pouch Upgrade and Gold Rupee.

Eldin Volcano

This Walkthrough for the Legend of Zelda: Skyward Sword contains data on Eldin Volcano, including planning for the excursion to Eldin, and how to get the Digging Mitts. Each progression is depicted with pictures and text, so you ought to have no issues exploring and finishing this mission. The mission and thing areas are something similar in Skyward Sword for Wii and Skyward Sword HD, however relying upon your control arrangement, bomb throws and a few fights might be simpler to finish in one rendition over the other.

The Eldin Volcano region fills in as the subsequent significant journey center point for Link's mission - in it, you're exploring magma overflowed regions, managing bringing down and raising stages, battling foes, and at last assembling every one of the Eldin Pieces of Key to enter the Earth Temple.

Planning for Eldin Volcano

Head back to Skyloft to squeeze the Ruby Tablet into the foundation of the Goddess Statue. Another Column of Light will open. Prior to making a beeline for Eldin Volcano, why not start some Side Quests? Here are the initial not many you can begin:

Lost Child

Pumpkin Landing

Missing Sister

You'll get some Heart Pieces, an Empty Bottle and different treats for finishing the Side Quests above. You may likewise need to visit Beedle's Shop. You can call down Beedle's Shop, coasting around the Bazaar, by focusing on its chime with a Beetle or Slingshot.

Significant

Make certain to purchase the Iron Shield from the Bazaar for 100 Rupees. This will not wreck in the blazing environs of Eldin Volcano. In the event that you wish, you can sell your Wooden Shield at the Item Check, yet it very well might be smarter to clutch it for some other time!

Additionally, purchase an Extra Wallet from Beedle. You'll rake in tons of cash where you are going, and you would prefer not to pass up Rupees on the grounds that your wallet is full! At last, an Adventure Pouch Upgrade might be all together too.

At the point when you are completely prepared, head to the new red section of light toward the north of Skyloft. This prompts Eldin Volcano. Eldin Volcano

At the point when you contact down in Eldin Volcano, Fi will caution you about bursting into flames. In the event that you actually have a Wooden Shield, you are nearly ensured to lose it here.

Get an Iron Shield, as of now. On the off chance that you burst into flames, you can roll or turn to drench the blazes.

Analyze the guide. Your way will be first toward the southwest corner, and afterward north from that point.

The Red Chuchus you experience can light you ablaze, so cut them up quick and utilize a Spin Attack on the little ones.

Goddess Cube

You can utilize Dowsing here to discover the way. The way toward the north prompts an impasse (and a divider you can bomb later) with little however a Volcanic Ladybug in it. Notwithstanding, close to the main Bird Statue is an edge with a Goddess Cube underneath it. This opens a chest in the most distant east of Skyloft with a Silver Rupee in it.

As you proceed down the way, Ledd and his companion will stop you. They will botch you as a foe and let you cruise by. After you interface with them, just prior to going into the cavern, look to one side, on the ground. You ought to have the option to see portions of the small plants. Drop off the precipice by then and you'll hit an edge, with a red rupee.

Utilize the plant to move back up. You'll go to a huge cavern loaded up with magma, Red Chuchus and Fire Keese. You can take out the Keese with your Slingshot or even the Beetle, however locking onto them and swinging in vertical movements is presumably the least demanding approach to move beyond them.

Run across the magma stages and advance southeast. In a lush collapse the far south, another Mogma will enlighten you concerning Bomb Flowers.

You can utilize Bomb Flowers to clear the stones around the entryway and furthermore over the little edge. Bombs, similar to Bomb Flowers, can be tossed by holding the Wii Remote up and afterward shaking it, or rolled, by pointing the Wii Remote down and afterward shaking it.

You can fold the bomb into the little entry here to clear a way to certain Rupees.

Throw a Bomb Flower upwards at the stones on the edge to take them out. Rupees are behind this mass of rocks, yet be careful with a goliath Chuchu behind another divider.

Roll a Bomb Flower into the Chuchu to explode it. An Amber Relic is in the little cottage, alongside a Volcanic Ladybug. In the event that you hurt yourself playing with bombs, sit on the stool in the cottage to recuperate.

Goddess Cube

Puncture the eastern divider to proceed. Follow the way east and somewhat north to discover another Goddess Cube in the southern focal part of Eldin Volcano. This opens a chest in the northwest of Skyloft with a Small Seed Satchel in it!

A little opening in the focal south region has rocks on the furthest finish of a passage. You can move a bomb through here to make the way. 20 Rupees are on the far side, and an Eldin Roller you can get also.

You can likewise send the Beetle up into the volcanic cone nearby to gather Hearts and Rupees.

Heart Piece

A Heart Piece is over the space toward the west, yet you can't grab it with the Beetle. All things being equal, send the Beetle past it and run it into a bomb by the shelled Pyrup. This should take it out so you can run right around and get the Heart Piece. On the off chance that you experience issues killing the Pyrup, it very well might be less difficult just allowed it to live and run past it when you arrive. Set a waypoint marker on your guide so you can explore your direction over to it.

A red beast, another Pyrup, will run into an opening and the ground as you advance east.

You can bowl a close by Bomb Flower into this opening to kill the Pyrup. Take out the Bokoblins and you'll go to a space with two shelled Pyrups.

You can take these out by throwing Bomb Flowers from the edge into the openings on their backs.

Cross this region and pull yourself up the edges to backtrack south to the Heart Piece.

In the following region, the red beasts are stowing away in skulls. You can throw bombs down at them from a higher place - throw them directly into the openings in the skulls.

There is a fragile scaffold gliding in the magma here with an impasse on the far side (a bomb-capable divider). Disregard this way for the time being and return to the weak extension.

You can move a Bomb Flower across it towards the magma ramble, snaring it somewhat left so it rolls into the stopped up opening in the far divider. This will turn off the opening and make steam spouts show up. Head straight for them.

Utilize the steam spout to get you into the fountain of liquid magma cone. From here you can hop off the edge and, as you fall, control your plunge to arrive on one of the numerous stages.

On the highest stage you can open a chest with Eldin Ore inside.

On another stage is a Goddess Cube, however it opens a chest in the Thunderhead which you can't reach yet.

On another stage are a few bombs. Land here and throw a bomb beneath at a break in the southern divider to discover a chest with a ultra uncommon Goddess Plume (or a Blue Bird Feather or Golden skull, especially uncommon things also) inside!

You can utilize a colossal steam spring in the upper east to return to the highest point of the cone and fall again and get the remainder of the plunder.

Save at the base at the Bird Statue. Toward the south is a Mogma who is overwhelmed by Bokoblins. It's an ideal opportunity to kill some Bokoblins.

There are a great deal of them - two Bokoblins with horns continue to call a lot of them. One is on the ground, another is on the stage in the corner. You need to ascend to his foundation and take him out.

The Mogma will be satisfied with your slaughter. He'll give you the Digging Mitts - which let you burrow at the X spots (Soft Soil).

On one of the stages in the Bokoblin room is a Treasure Chest that you can't reach yet. Along these lines, disregard it until further notice.

All things considered, search for a dive spot in the room and burrow on it to make a steam ramble show up. Ride on it to another burrow where you can over and over burrow on it for Rupees and, perhaps, some Eldin Ore until you can burrow on it no more.

Tip: Be certain to burrow at each opening to get Rupees, Hearts and every so often Eldin Ore.

Drop down and go behind the Mogma, who gave you the Digging Mitts, and burrow on the burrow spot behind him to make another steam ramble show up. Go up on it and you will see the way split into two . Take the way on the left and burrow at the burrow spot at the impasse to make one more steam ramble show up.

Go up it and ascend the stepping stool. You will presently be in a space where the Bokoblins seem to have camped out at. Take out the independent Bokoblin here and look to one side to see three chutes.

Take the center chute to slide to the chest that was referenced before for an Eldin Ore piece.

Return to where the way parts into two and take the way on the at this moment. You will be in a room with numerous Pyrups, stowing away in little passages, obstructing your way. You'll discover some Bomb Plants along the western divider in an alcove just as along the eastern divider in the southern corner. Use them to get out close by Pyrups by folding the bombs into their fire spouts. Presently, utilize a Bomb Plant to clear the broke divider in the north - you can see the niche on your guide. Inside is a Chest with a Silver Rupee!

Utilize the Bomb Plants to kill the entirety of the Pyrups nearby and head out the eastern exit.

Dive in the following space to track down a little steam ramble. Gather the Amber Relic and afterward utilize the steam spout to get to a tremendous steam ramble that will get you back to the surface.

Approach Ledd and he will reveal to you that an individual like you, dressed all in dark, came charging through. Go to one side and make the impeded way with the solitary Bomb Plant to make an easy route back toward the southeast region.

Presently, head for goliath hole. The scaffold will naturally interface when you draw near, and you will experience Impa interestingly. She reveals to you that Zelda is simply ahead and to rush. Pass through the door and look to one side to see some Bomb Plants and a separated pinnacle.

Take a Bomb Plant and spot it behind the separated pinnacle at a broke piece of the divider to uncover a chest that contains a Red Rupee in it. After you do that, save at the Bird Statue.

Follow the northern way, killing the two Fire Keese en route, to the huge, sandy slope. Run up the precarious edge and stop at the stage to wipe out the solitary Bokoblin.

Cross the sand to another stage and utilize a Bomb Flower to make the obstructed way underneath - this will make an alternate way back toward the southeast.

Return to the stage you battled the solitary Bokoblin on and nail the Bokoblin moving stones with the Slingshot. Try to point over its head so you will hit it (in the event that you need Deku Seeds, there is a burrow spot on the other stage that contains them).

Presently you can move up to the top. At the highest point of the slope is a shoddy town.

A Bokoblin in a high pinnacle here is blowing his horn happily. Bomb his pinnacle with a close by bomb plant.

This will make a scaffold across. Prior to intersection, you might need to look at Thrill Digger, a toss of the dice, past a Bomb Wall behind one of the cabins here.

Snatch the Sacred Relic and climb the mass of plants. The monster red Chu-Chus up here should be cleaved into more modest Chu-Chus before they can be annihilated.

Run up the lofty slope and stop on the principal level stage to stay away from the rocks. Utilize the stages to shoot Slingshot pellets at the rock moving Bokoblins and get up the slope securely. A bomb-capable divider is in favor of this slope, yet you can't open it yet.

After the cutscene with the Mogmas you'll have the Dowsing capacity you need to discover five Pieces of Key. Note that in this space you can get the Eldin Roller for your Bug Collection.

Goddess Cube

Likewise, toward the west of the locked entryway is a burrow spot which uncovered a steam spring. You can convey a Bomb Flower over to it and step in to bring the bomb up to the Bomb-capable Wall. Past it is a Goddess Cube. This opens a chest on Bamboo Island with a Gold Rupee inside.

Goddess Cube

Toward the east of the locked entryway is a Bokoblin Village with a pinnacle in it you can bomb to make a scaffold. Rather than intersection the scaffold, search for a way driving down to one side of it, ending in this not entirely obvious Goddess Cube. This opens a chest in the upper east of Skyloft with the extre

The Pieces of Key

This piece of our Walkthrough for the Legend of Zelda: Skyward Sword and Skyward Sword HD guides you from Eldin Volcano's prison to the Earth Temple, by showing you where to track down every one of the

Pieces of Key.

After you complete the Eldin Volcano principle center, you will track down that the Earth Temple's passageway is locked. You'll require five Pieces of Key to open the riddle lock. Your splashing capacity assists you with finding the key sections, yet we make it much simpler for you by showing you every one of the areas:

First Piece of Key

Only west of the principle entryway in a burrow spot. Inside is a Piece of Key.

Second Piece of Key

Only east of the principle entryway is an overlaid flight of stairs. There are some Bomb Flowers on the edge of the incline.

Utilize these to bomb the divider on the east side of the incline. Run to the bombarded divider and burrow for the Piece of Key.

Third Piece of Key

One is further west of the entryway. You will see an incline toward the southwest of the fundamental entryway. Roll a bomb down the incline to push over the pinnacle.

Slide down and burrow there for the Piece of Key. Run back up the incline to get back to the entryway region.

Fourth Piece of Key

Toward the upper east of the locked entryway (utilize the wrecked pinnacle connect) is a slope sitting above a mass of plants. You need to drop down and hurry along an edge to one side towards a Heart Plant.

Follow this way up and afterward utilize the edge to leap to a higher edge. From here, hop across to the plant divider. Rapidly move right and, on the off chance that you need it, get the Stamina Fruit. At the top, hit the catch to broaden the extension.

There's an extreme warmth region here which will light you ablaze - yet you need to go through here, notwithstanding the danger. Simply don't go higher up yet (that is a later journey). In this way, for the time being, head into the superheated region and race to one side and down the slide. You can move while heading to extinguish the fire and diminish harm.

You can get a few treats on this slide and pick a left and a correct way (you ought to do both), yet you'll need to get back to the highest point of the slide for the Piece of Key.

Goddess Cube

Take the left side and Aim for the left stage with a Dig Spot on it. Underneath this is another stage with a Goddess Cube on it.

Note that the stage on the right as you slide down has a Pink Fairy on it in a Dig Spot.

At the base, you can bomb a divider to make an alternate way back toward the south. Take the enormous fountain back up to the highest point of the slide here. This time, take the correct way for an arrival far underneath.

A Pink Fairy can be found in the burrows spot on the stage you come to first.

Keep sliding to one side and you will go to a subsequent stage (presented previously). Two springs are simply off the left edge of this stage. You need to time this leap impeccably.

Trust that the far spring will ramble prior to bouncing. This will get you to the following Eldin Piece of Key in a burrow spot on the stage.

Fifth Piece of Key

To track down the last piece of key for the Earth Temple/Eldin Volcano: at the lower part of the long slide is a passage driving north to a cavern with a sandy grade and a magma pool.

Toward one side is a module the divider (pivot once you enter the cavern). You can throw a bomb at this fitting. To do this, run up over the attachment with a bomb blossom and throw it down.

Presently, with the magma filled in, you can throw one more bomb at a bomb-capable divider. BOWL this bomb at the divider. Inside is the last Piece of Key.

Head to the prison entrance with the five Key Pieces and the entryway will open. You would now be able to get to the Earth Temple.

Earth Temple

Cross the little stages in the primary space to get to a bunch of blue steps. In the event that you go to one side and cross the stages, there a few burrow spots there (one of the spots contains a Red Chuchu) just as the Mogma that is consistently with Ledd. Converse with him and he discloses to you that Ledd has disappeared.

Return to the arrangement of blue steps and look to one side of the steps to detect a burrow spot on the ground.

Burrow here to make a spring ramble that prompts a Chest with a Red Rupee inside it.

Go to the steps and trust that the magma will quit erupting up the stage before you. Bounce on the stage when it's down and leap to the next one trusting that the magma will lift it up. At the point when it's up, leap to the ground and you will come to what in particular seems, by all accounts, to be an impasse.

To one side and the right, there are two pinion wheels that have ropes on that that you can cut. Cut descending upward on the ropes to cut them. Doing as such will to some degree open an entryway.

There is one final stuff close to the entryway on the right side. This one must be cut by the Beetle. Pilot your Beetle ready and cut it with the pliers to open the way north.

There is a red Rupee on the upper left half of the entryway.

A Lizalfo is on the far side. This is a truly extreme adversary in case you're not used to its battling style. In the event that you swing uncontrollably, it will hinder everything. The way in to this battle is to counter its assaults with your Iron Shield.

Lock on and sit tight for it to assault, then, at that point push the nunchuk forward and counter its assault with a Shield Bash. This will leave it open to your assaults.

Periodically, the Lizalfo will insult you with its watched arm over its head. At the point when it does this, wound it with a forward push, or a slice from the bearing inverse of where it's guarding, and afterward whack it some more to polish it off. A high level move, on the off chance that you notice the Lizalfo hopping back to inhale fire (yet not bouncing back to hit you with his tail, in which case you should Shield Bash all things being equal), you can attempt a leap assault.

While Z-focusing on, move towards the Lizalfo and press A to bounce. While in mid-air, do an upward slice to wreck it. In the event that you wreck the Lizalfo, you can utilize a Fatal Blow to effortlessly polish it off. A leap assault and Fatal Blow can complete a Lizalfo in two hits!

After the Lizalfo is dealt with, shoot the Bomb Flowers on the huge sculpture coasting in the magma with your slingshot or hit one of them with your Beetle.

Its eyeball will move into the magma. You can jump onto the eyeball and use it to move to the focal stage. The eyeball will move insofar as you run on it, however in the event that you start to sneak off the side, quit running and you will re-focus.

The Magma Spumes here ought to be kept away from ashore, yet you can utilize the eyeball to turn over them and kill them. Save at the Bird Statue in the center island of the room.

Note: There is a dive spot in the center island that contains Hearts in case you are coming up short on wellbeing.

Presently, roll the eyeball to left half of the Lizalfo room. Bounce on the stage here WITH a bomb and throw it at the obstructed region above, or throw a bomb on the stage and let it accomplish practically everything for you.

A last technique is to bounce on the stage, put the bomb down, and hop ease off the stage once more. A Golden Skull can be found in a Chest up here.

Get back on the eyeball and roll north through the openings in the messed up connect.
A Chest on the far side has a Blue Bird Feather in it. You can likewise burrow here for Eldin Ore and get an Amber Relic.

A "gear-tooth" on the focal scaffold is standing out in the magma. You can fold the eyeball into the gear-tooth on the northwest side to push the machine gear-piece in and raise one of two extension parts.

A sculpture is impeding the eyeball's way toward the upper east, so get off on the eastern edge and converse with Ledd the Mogma.

He's recognized his lost Bomb Bag on the furthest side of the impeded rocks, sweet!

Creep under the fence utilizing the opening by the hindered divider. Bowl a bomb under the fence utilizing the opening and you ought to have the option to blow open the divider.

Prior to leaving, creep up the stepping stool around here and cross the flimsy portion of fence to discover some Dig Spots and one of them contains a Pink Fairy.

Get back to Ledd and enter the eastern entryway. This is an intense battle. One Lizalfo will generally ease off permitting you to zero in on one. At the point when this occurs, utilize your Shield Bash and hits to take out each Lizalfo.

Your award is the Bomb Bag - yet you'll have to converse with Ledd before you can utilize it. At the point when you leave the room, you will converse with Ledd and he will give you the Bomb Bag and five Bombs to kick you off.

You can utilize Bombs similar as Bomb Plants, yet you'll have the option to convey an inventory with you consistently. Additionally, Bombs pulled from your Bomb Bag don't have a lit breaker until you let go of them!

To get more bombs, you can get Bomb Plants and stuff them in your Bomb Sack. To do as such, approach a Bomb Plant and press the A catch to get it. Then, at that point, press the B catch to supply it in the Bomb Bag.

Get back on the eyeball. Roll it upper east to the messed up section. Here you can BARELY make out a broke divider toward the east. Throw bombs at it - it will take different attempts - and you can blow it open.

Roll past the mythical beast mouths regurgitating fire and search for one more broke divider at the impasse before the subsequent winged serpent mouth. You can see it on your guide also. Bomb it and roll through the entry to track down a protected spot to arrive on.

Note: Look up to discover a winged serpent's mouth high on the divider that isn't regurgitating magma. Utilize the bug to explore into the mouth and through the passage to track down a silver rupee.

Get off and fire your Beetle through the passage by the Bird Statue. On the other side of the huge red door is a rope switch you can cut with the creepy crawly. Another is as an afterthought confronting you. Chopping both will cut down the door.

Roll through the entryway and you can get off on the far side and back track to the Bird Statue and save.

Roll across the problematic magma way. You can get off on a stage with a Lizalfo to score a Red Rupee Chest.

Back in the enormous room, you will currently approach the subsequent machine gear-piece. Roll into it to open the entryway. You would now be able to land on the center stage. Use the stairwell that lead to the entryway in the west.

Get the Amber Relic to one side of the passage. In this room, basically cross the stages toward the west and ride the last one up on a crest of magma to get the Dungeon Map!

Head once again into the focal chamber and continue through the now open way toward the north.

You'll go to an enormous slope driving north. Run up the incline and creep into the niche on the passed on to let the stones moves securely past you.

At the lower part of the following incline, search for a little opening you can slither through on the right side. Delve in the Dig Spot on the far side and ride the spring up to the edge.

You can run up the steps here and throw Bombs down at the Bomb-capable Wall. Focus on the obvious blemish on the floor and it will move down and unlock the divider.

Presently you can run up the incline, taking shelter in the besieged out niche.

A huge winged serpent head is at the top. Save at the Bird Statue and afterward run up the steps.

The incline above is so long you'll have to utilize organic product to get to the Chest at the top with the Dragon Sculpture (Boss Key) inside.

Sadly, the sanctuary goes all Indiana Jones on you for snatching the Dragon Sculpture. Prior to running down the slope, seek the appropriate for a Goddes Plume.

Run down the slope right to the lower part of the way to send the rock flying into the mythical beast's mouth.

In the event that you delayed down and get run over, it's Game Over, so be careful!

At the manager entryway, make the key resemble a lowercase "d" and spot it in the lock.

Head up the steps and get ready for a battle. Get a few Bombs and pocket them until your Bomb Bag is full.

Run up the long slope and Ghirahim will stand up to you once more.

Pyroclastic Fiend Scaldera

After the cutscene, flee from the monster, pivoting to throw a Bomb in its open mouth.

You will likely push it way down the slope by throwing Bombs at it. You can possibly hit him when his blazes are drenched out - typically one Bomb is sufficient to thump Scaldera to the base.

At the point when it arrives at the base, it will suck in air fully expecting a fireball assault. Throw a Bomb at it and it will suck it in and explode, losing a portion of its shell and tumbling to the ground with its flimsy point uncovered.

Quickly approach it and slice the shaky area, the eye. Presently, flee and prepare to rehash this interaction.

You will just have to switch things around infrequently. Now and then Scaldera will raise up on its legs and abandon above you. Remain under it and let it disregard you, then, at that point avoid it to one side or right as it moves down.

You can keep Scaldera under control with only 10 bombs and some master moves, yet in the event that you need more, race to the actual top of the slope and stock up. You'll need to keep an eye out for fireballs up here, yet Scaldera can not pass the Bomb Plants on the slope. There are Hearts up here too.

Eliminating Scaldera's defensive layer makes it simpler to hit its shaky area, however just direct harm to the eye will kill the monster.

After you rout Scaldera, snatch your Heart Container and head to the highest point of the slope.

Earth Spring

In the Earth Spring, you will have a concise experience with Zelda in a cutscene. After it's done, you can snatch a Pink Fairy or three by the cascades. Other than that, the solitary thing left to do is approach the change and hit the wing image with a Skyward Strike.

You'll get the Amber Tablet. You realize what to do - back to Skyloft! In the Statue of the Goddess, fit the Amber Tablet into spot and it will open an entryway to Lanayru Desert.
Lanayru Mine

Goddess Cube

At the point when you land in Lanayru there is an edge around the space with a chest on it - you can't get this currently, yet you'll have the option to get up to the edge with a thing you find later.

For the time being you can gather a Goddess Cube behind the stage you land on. This opens a Silver Rupee chest northwest of Skyloft. Overlook the old robots until further notice.

You can likewise load up on bombs back here. The stone heaps in the space hold a few rupees. There is additionally a Sand Cicada on the rear of the column on the off chance that you wish to get it.

Head north and push the mine truck down the track so it tumbles off the edge. Presently, pull it to the far side and go through it to climb the edge.

The Yellow Chuchus here convey intermittent electric shocks and very irritating. Just cut them between shocks.

Bigger variants of the Yellow Chuchu will swallow Bombs, exploding quickly a while later. Utilize this to monitor hearts.

In the following clearing, gather Rupees with your Beetle, then, at that point whack the gem nearby.

This is a Timeshift Stone, and it will change a little segment of the desert to its previous lavishness and energy. These are found all through Lanayru and are utilized to settle a wide range of riddles.

The LD-301 robots in the space will spring up within the sight of the Timeshift Stone. You can converse with them prior to continuing on. In the middle of the transport lines toward the west is an uncommon, helpful Treasure, the Ancient Flower.

These just show up in the time bubbles left by Timeshift Stones. Bounce in the mine truck nearby and it will take you through a way toward the north for a Red Rupee Chest.

The other mine truck track must be utilized in the event that you drive the mine truck from the east into the time bubble.

Jump in it to continue south. Toward the finish of the mine truck track will be one more Ancient Flower.

Discussing Timeshift Stones, there is another in this room, yet it is under a heap of rocks.

Bomb the stones and whack it to bring the room into its own time bubble. The sculpture on the divider has a vessel that a bomb fits impeccably into.

Toss a Bomb into this vessel and the sculpture will crash and burn, permitting you to continue toward the west.

Four a greater amount of these sculptures lie in the sandpit toward the east. This sand trap is very risky.

It will suck you in the event that you don't run, however running saps your Stamina Guage fundamentally. This implies you should hurry to close safe spots and recuperate to cross the sand trap.

To make a protected spot (or four), bomb the sculptures in the corridor.

Behind one on the north side is an opening prompting a room with a Red Rupee Chest.

There are additionally Lanayru Ants stowing away in the containers for your bug assortment.

The sandy corridor prompts a bigger sand trap room with Electro Spumes in it. To kill Electro Spumes rapidly, simply bowl a Bomb at them.

You can cross this room utilizing the islands. Just race to the closest island and re-energize, then, at that point race to the close to cross the void.

You can return in no time for the Chest on the high stage.

Run up the slope and hang a left. The sand trap filled entry toward the west has a few bunches of rocks in it.

You can bowl Bombs at the stone clusters to explode them and uncover a Timeshift Stone somewhere far off.

Exploding the stones around it will likewise initiate the Timeshift Stone.

This will fill the sand trap with grass and make it crossable. In transit across, get the Ancient Flower. As you stroll down the passageway notice there are two Gerudo Dragonflies to get. A short time later, you would now be able to advance toward the Chest in the south, which holds an alternate thing for each game.

It has been known to get the absolute most uncommon collectables, for example, a Blue Bird Feather, a Goddess Plume, or a Golden Skull. Stunningly better, ANOTHER Ancient Flower can be discovered developing behind the chest stage!

In the enormous sand trap room that is somewhat in the past now, there is a mine truck you can push in to the Timeshift Stone air pocket and afterward ride north.

Lanayru Desert

Save at the Bird Statue in the southern corner of the desert. The stones around the mine truck track hold a Timeshift Stone.

Enact the stone to make a few plants on the eastern divider. Climb the plants to track down an Ancient Flower.

Utilize the hand grasps to hurry across further toward the west and you'll track down a little cavern prompting a Chest with an arbitrary uncommon thing (Blue Bird Feather, Goddess Plume, or Golden Skull) inside.

Sweet! Subsequent to leaving the cavern, to one side will be 3 Lanaryu Ants. Note that theres is an article covered in the sand above also.

You'll have to return here for a Side Quest to get Fun Island functional a lot later.

Drop down into the bowl underneath. It is loaded up with Ampilus foes - genuinely impressive moving electric shells. You have a couple of choices for killing them. One is to hit the red part of the Amplius when it rises out of its shell at a huge span with your Slingshot.

This will shock it, permitting you to get right up front and cut it to death. Another strategy is to shock its accusing assault of your safeguard. You should time your nunchuk poke consummately to daze it - and, obviously, don't endeavor this with the Iron Shield. Another might be to remain close to a divider and evade before it hits hit you. It will be dazed and effectively killable.

Additionally in this space you'll periodically recognize the unimaginably accommodating Tumbleweed. You can pick these up with your Bug Net

- they are a helpful Treasure for overhauls.

A Chest on one of the dividers toward the north contains a Tumbleweed too. You can't get the Goddess Cube here now, so center around the two pens by the divider here.

You can utilize the situation on the divider by the Chest to get on one of the enclosures.

From here you can throw bombs into a confine and uncover a Timeshift Stone.

Throw another bomb in to actuate it. This will make a lavish air pocket around the enclosures, uncovering two Technoblins.

These adversaries have electrical nudges, which you would prefer not to connect with. A counter from your safeguard should assist with making them helpless against assaults. Then again, a Slingshot pellet can daze them.

When you kill the entirety of the Technoblins, converse with the robot in the enclosure and he'll give you the Hook Beetle.

This exceptionally marvelous move up to the Beetle permits it to get things and drop them. You can get Bombs now, which is an extremely valuable procedure for killing foes.

For the present, look at the sand trap areas toward the west. You ought to recognize the figures with bomb vessels in them coating the sand. To get bombs into the containers these sculptures hold you should utilize the Hook Beetle.
Send it towards the highest points of the trees close by with Bomb Plants developing on their dry branches. Get the Bomb by flying into it, then, at that point head for one of the sculptures.

Hit Z on the nunchuck to switch points while flying a you can without much of a stretch drop bombs into the containers. Utilize this method to make a way across the sand trap.

In the following region you can swipe a Bomb Plant with the Hook Beetle and smash it into the goliath, irritating birds called Hroks.

Goddess Cube

The Ampilus shells can be utilized as venturing stones in the southeast ocean of sand. Utilize the Hook Beetle to hit them with bombs - however stay far away. They are just helpful as venturing stones in case they are in their beginning positions.

Have persistence for the Ampilus to stroll around nearer to your area. You ought to have the option to scarcely come to each Ampilus shell.

Utilize this strategy to arrive at the Goddess Cube on the southern side of the space. This opens a chest south of Skyloft with a Heart Medal inside. This will be fundamental for use in Hero Mode.

Cross the sand ocean and save at the Bird Statue. You can back track along the edge here to drive a mine truck into an advantageous situation for an alternate way.

The following sand ocean has a momentum that will convey the Ampilus shells - with you on them. Nail the animals with Hook Beetle Bombs and you can ride the shell to the far off islands.

Indeed, you can back track along the edge of the level to get to a mine truck that can be driven into an alternate route position.

Enter the eastern way to get to the Temple of Time.

Sanctuary of Time (Exterior)

Save at the Desert Gorge Bird Statue. Search for a Timeshift Stone on a rough highlight the north. You can hit this with the Hook Beetle to make an extension across the canyon.

Utilize the Beetle to hack down any Deku Babas in the manner and afterward kill the Technoblin on the center stage.

You can gather an Ancient Flower here, and another Ancient Flower on a stage toward the east - simply send your Beetle to recover it!

Presently, send the Hook Beetle inside the spring of gushing lava like cone toward the west and hit the pink change to open the entryway inside.

Send the Hook Beetle to the actual top of the cone with a Bomb and let it straight fall down (hold Z and afterward press A) the cone to hit a Timeshift Stone. Presently you can utilize the mine truck to cross to the far west. Watch out for a Deku Baba on the roof of the well of lava cone.

Your old buddy Gorko is on the opposite side by the fell access to the Temple of Time.

Converse with him and afterward utilize the Hook Beetle to convey bombs up to the highest points of the towers with rock bunches on them toward the north.

Under one of these is a Timeshift Stone. Actuate it and you'll see a robot in the way of a mine truck. You'll need to kill the Technoblins nearby to move the robot.

The robot won't just move, yet in addition "update" your guide to show past structures nearby toward the east.

This aides monstrously, in light of the fact that it shows the designs clouded by sand you can securely stroll on without sinking!

Goddess Cube

Push or ride the mine truck to the edge of the Timeshift Stone's impact. Another Stone is across the crevasse. Actuate this with the Hook Beetle and get in the mine truck.

Charge a Skyward Strike and hit the Goddess Cube as the mine truck passes it. You would prefer not to miss this one, either, since a Heart Piece is inside the chest it opens on Beedle's Island in the upper east of the sky.

Prior to leaving through the space's northeastern entryway, send the Beetle up to the Timeshift Stone over the space to make a little green stage toward the south. Send the Beetle here to get the Ancient Flower.

The Generator

Back in the Lanayru Desert focal region, analyze your guide and leave onto the sand in a space that shows a lowered divider (dim lines). Fi should reach you and educate you regarding the lowered construction and furthermore overhaul your guide so you can add more waypoints.

To navigate this region securely, put waypoints at corner of the lowered design and spot them along the constructions lines.

Follow the shining blue spots to cross the desert without any problem. Get on the uncovered divider in the east and go around toward the north to save at the Bird Statue.

Close to the Bird Statue is a Timeshift Stone under a heap of rocks. Hit it to actuate a period bubble that envelopes the Generator in the focal point of the space.

A robot close to it will give you the wretched: there are three Power Nodes that should be enacted close by to get the generator rolling. You can Dowse to discover them.

Just beneath the robot is an Ancient Flower. You can snatch this while heading to the principal Power Node.

Force Node 1

Advance west first Dowsing to discover a column of sculptures along a divider. On the off chance that you bomb the center one (utilize the Hook Beetle to drop a Bomb Plant on it) you can uncover the primary Power Node.

To actuate the Power Node, stick your sword into it by utilizing a wounding movement. Pivot the Wii Remote to one side to turn the Power Node's dial and actuate it. An image will currently show up on your guide.

Force Node 2

This Power Node is in a cavern close to the Bird Statue in the focal point of the space. Search for a break on the divider toward the north and utilize a Bomb to uncover the passageway to an antiquated distribution center.

Try not to try and endeavor to cross the sand here. The Ampilus foes here are difficult to pass. All things being equal, carry a Bomb out to the center heap of rocks. This will uncover a Timeshift Stone. Hit this and the sand will be taken out from the space.

Moreover, Technoblins will be going around the floor underneath, and the Ampilus will be diminished to [[Ampilus Egg]]s. These can be conveyed with your Hook Beetle securely.

For the time being, work on getting out the Technoblins and getting together the two Rupee Chests along the west side of the floor. Make sure to utilize your Slingshot to stagger the Technoblins.

In the most distant north of the room is a foot switch that opens a little board you can put an Ampilus Egg in. This will open the secondary passage.

Inside you'll discover Power Node 2. Wound it and turn the wrench counterclockwise. With this Node actuated, don't leave the back room presently - there's a Chest up above!

Send the Hook Beetle out to the Timeshift Stone and hit it and the room will load up with sand. It will kill you, however it will likewise store you on an edge above. Open the Chest for a Blue Feather.

Utilize the Beetle to hit the Timeshift Stone again and you can leave the little room. Cross the room and leave the distribution center.

Force Node 3

To will Power Node 3 you'll need to utilize your guide markers adequately. The example of antiquated dividers structure three concentric rings around a focal sand pit.

As you work your direction east from the Bird Statue by Node 2, mark a way on the center ring so you can cross it. You'll require the Claw Shot to get the Goddess Cube in the north, so return later.

The eastern desert has a switch that will open an easy route back to the beginning region in the south. Prior to heading in the entryway by the Bird Statue, search for the Sand Cicada on the back side of the construction.

Sneak up on it and grab it with the Bug Net - this is an uncommon bug you can generally get here. The Gerudo Dragonfly can be found close by, as well, and the Lanayru Ant is in burrow spots close to the Sand Cicada area.

At long last, an Amber Relic can be found on the structure. Gather it with the Beetle.

Inside the structure is another sandy distribution center loaded up with Ampilus adversaries. Bowl a bomb into the closest one and advance out onto the protected spots in the sand.

By and by the focal cluster of rocks conceals a Timeshift Stone. Explode it, however don't enact the stone.

You need to get to the furthest side of the sand stream, and since there's a current, you can ride an Ampilus shell across. Try to kill the Ampilus on the furthest side of the Timeshift Stone while it's both close by and in a situation to stream to the far side.

Stay away so it doesn't see you and attempt to utilize a Bomb to handicap it. In the event that you remain by the stone, you might have the option to hit with your blade in the event that it rolls at you and gets shocked. An extremely lethargic approach to kill it is to send charged Skyward Strikes at it.

Get on the shell and take it to the far side. Move up on the crates along the western divider and run back toward the south.

Open the Chest for some Eldin Ore. Push the case close to the chest off the edge of the carton heap to make a way up, then, at that point hit the Timeshift Stone to deplete the sand.

You would now be able to investigate the ground level, killing Technoblins with your Slingshot and blade and gathering the two minor Rupee chests.

Here you'll discover Ampilus Eggs. Utilize the Beetle to convey it to the most distant side of the huge chasm and drop it close to the little container that controls the locked entryway, very much as you accomplished for Node 2.

Move up on the western containers and cross the region. Here you can remain on the foot switch and push the Egg into the container to control the entryway.

On the opposite side of the locked entryway is a Chest with a Monster Horn inside and another with a Blue Rupee.

Cut your blade into the Power Node and wrench it to one side. You should now have three imprints on your guide, one image for each Power Node.

The time has come to get back to the Generator in the focal point of the northern area of the desert. Hit the Timeshift Stone and approach it.

Note that you can sit on the stool to one side of the Generator to recuperate your hearts.

With 3 Power Nodes running, you would now be able to settle the riddle of the Generator. The key is the images on the guide in the Power Node areas. You need to turn the wrench to the blue, yellow and orange images match their situations on the guide. The format is like a clock, so here are the right positions:

Blue (Water) - 9 O'Clock

Orange (Fire) - 4 O'Clock

Yellow (Bolt) - 12 O'Clock

With the images in these positions, the Lanayru Mining Facility will emerge from the desert. Note that this design makes an easy route back to the wide range of various pieces of the desert. Climb the northern steps to discover the passageway to the Mine.

Lanayru Mining Facility

The section region is loaded up with Arachas, little scorpion-like animals you'll be seeing a great deal of in the Mining Facility. You can kill them in one blow, yet when they group up they can be interesting. Twist Attacks prove to be useful when they swarm you. You should see in the northern corners of the room are two switches you can run up the divider and get.

There are sand pits before each of these, and Electro Spumes in them. The northwest pit has a sculpture with a Bomb-sized bin in it. A Bomb Plant is developing on a column in the room. Fly the Beetle to the Bomb Plant and convey the Bomb to the bin in the sculpture. You should hold Z on the nunchuk and afterward press A to drop the bomb. This will make a protected zone across the sand for you to remain on. You can likewise bomb the Electro Spumes utilizing the Beetle.

Race to the fallen sculpture and actuate the switch. This makes the way for the north. To get to the switch on the upper east side, you'll need to just stumble into the sand. Utilize a mix of running and short strolls to arrive at the opposite side - this will delay the measure of time you can spend crossing the sand. Pull the change to open a door on the east side of the room with a Red Rupee Chest inside. You can likewise toss bombs in the sculptures that line the dividers to get to a couple of more Rupees.

Head north through the entryway. There are two locked entryways here, one which requires a Small Key. This is the thing that you will be looking for straightaway. Staldra monitor the two sides of the way. Make sure to thump them back with your safeguard when they assault to effectively daze them. Cut each head in one swipe to dispense with them.

On the left half of the brought region up in the north are containers you can push around to make a way up to the entryway. Push a box against the divider and run up it. Head through the northern entryway.

The monstrous focal corridor of the Lanayru Mining Facility is totally closed off, beside a way toward the east. Save at the Bird Statue and afterward search for a Bomb Plant on a column.

Send your Beetle to recover the bomb and afterward drop it onto the heap of boxes toward the east. This will open a way. Bomb the Yellow Chuchu from a good ways and afterward bounce across the little island to the stepping stool.

Be careful with the Thunder Keese here which promptly assault you at the highest point of the stepping stool. These Keese are intense, however you can generally obstruct them with a Shield (inasmuch as it isn't the Iron Shield).

Up here is a Chest with a Small Key in it. Get back toward the southern corridor with the locked entryway (set apart on your guide) and open it to get to the eastern lobby.

This sand-filled region is overflowing with Froaks, drifting hazardous adversaries that can undoubtedly be exploded with your Slingshot. The Beetle is a clumsier, yet reasonable, choice too.

Cross the dead transport line and climb the weeds on the far side. From here you can ascend a stepping stool to arrive at a story switch toward the edge of the room; yet the stepping stool is hindered by a box.

A Bomb Plant develops high on the passageway to the room, fortunately, and you can get the Bomb and drop it on the case.

Move up and remain on the floor switch. This will open a chamber with a Timeshift Stone in the focal point of the sandy pit. Send your Beetle for it. When you leave the switch the Timeshift Stone will be hindered once more, but enacted.

Drop down and face your first Beamos. These enemies should ALWAYS be drawn nearer while their eye faces from you. The bar they radiate will rapidly dissolve your Shield, so be careful! To take them out quickly, approach the base and swipe at it evenly to chop it down a level - some Beamos are tall and will expect you to remove a few areas. At the point when the Beamos is brought down to your stature, cut its eye with a pushing movement of the Wii Remote to polish it off.

You can run across the part of red transport line here. At the point when you arrive at the following belt, you'll need to cross the space toward the north. Run across the red transport line, keeping away from the stones and getting the Stamina Fruit. It's simpler than it sounds!

This prompts a few inclines that will take you to a locked entryway and another transport line. At the most distant finish of this belt is a Beamos and a divider switch. Yank this change to open the locked entryway you just passed. Drop off the edge and you can pull another divider switch beneath.

This will get you admittance to a Red Rupee Chest on the north side of the room. Cross the transport line toward the north side once more, snatch the Chest and afterward exit through the opened entryway.

In the following room are many, numerous stages and spikes lining a significant part of the floor, keeping you from getting toward the northern stage, with the Gust Bellows in it. To arrive, you'll need to take a course over the spikes, utilizing the stages.

To start with, leap toward the southeastern stage and point a Slingshot pellet at the Froak by the heap of rocks. It ought to explode, clearing the stones and making it protected to travel north. Cross the stages to the stepping stool in the north and climb it to discover the Gust Bellows!

This air-rambling gadget will get little heaps free from sand, uncovering switches and fortunes, blow numerous foes away and furthermore influence propeller-driven gadgets!

You can test it on the sand heaps nearby. In particular, blow the Froak in the northwest corner into the heap of rocks to make a way toward the western entryway.

By the stepping stool prompting this entryway is a square you can push to the ground to make an alternate route. Do as such, then, at that point search for a Chest on the ground with a Rare Item (Goddess Plume, Blue Bird Feather, or Golden Skull) inside!

The western entryway is obstructed by sand heaps. Blow them away with the Gust Bellows and head through the entryway.

Back in the focal lobby, push the square far removed and you can move down the stepping stool. Save at the Bird Statue.

Head south one room. Here one entryway remains locked. The change to open it is under a heap of sand in the upper east corner of the room. Blow the entirety of the sand away, killing the Arachas as they show up.

Push the square onto the floor switch that shows up and the way toward the west will be open.

The sandy western lobby holds confidential under a heap of sand in the southeast corner. Advance over to this, blowing the Froaks to the side.

Utilize the Gust Bellows to clear the sand and you will discover a Timeshift Stone. Smack it and analyze the new environmental factors. There are a few breeze controlled stages in the room. You can move these by passing the Gust Bellows wind stream more than one side. You can make them go both ways, contingent upon the side you blow.

Be mindful so as not to blow a stage far away or you'll need to hit the Timeshift Stone again to go to it in the sand.

You can utilize the focal breeze fueled stage to arrive at the Chest with a Monster Horn inside.

An entryway on the south side of the room would now be able to be opened, also. The time bubble uncovers a fan over the door which you can point the Gust Bellows at. Do as such and you will actually want to raise the entryway.

In spite of the fact that you can undoubtedly deal with the Beamos on the opposite side, another sort of foe, the Sentrobe ought to be a bit trickier. The Sentrobe has two methods of assault. For the primary mode, you need to send its shots back at it. You can do this with a coordinated Shield counter assault (best) or with an upward swipe of the blade.

After you hit the Sentrobe. it will change modes and fire two tests at you. One of this has an upward blue line, the other a level blue line. These are the creases you can swipe to deliver them in twain. Slice them both down the middle and get back to the Shield strategy. hit it again and it will shower the room in Rupees, the vast majority of which will fall into the void.

The room's exit is simply ahead. To arrive at it, utilize the Gust Bellows to push the stage to one side, permitting you to bounce on it. From the stage, utilize the breeze of your Bellows to push it back to its beginning spot, so you can get off on the opposite side.

The entryway driving out toward the north is protected by a Beamos. It is additionally locked with a windmill lock. Utilize the Gust Bellows to open it.

This room has some intense foes in it. The two Staldra are recognizable, yet ensure you draw one away from the other prior to assaulting it.

Clear the sand heaps around the square on the north side of the room and push it right toward the west. Climb the square and glance through the door on the upper level. There is a heap of sand clouding a Timeshift Stone here. Hit the stone with the Slingshot and the Armos beneath will wake up.

The Armos is incredibly risky on the off chance that you don't stay away. The secret to this odd gadget is to turn the highest point of its head with the Gust Bellows. Doing as such will open its mouth and stagger it. There are two blue flimsy parts in its mouth. Once can be swiped with an even cut, however the other, more troublesome one to hit should be cut with a push movement.

Kill the Armos to open the entryway above with the Chest behind it AND the entryway driving east. The Chest contains the Dungeon Map!

Note that an Amber Relic can be found on one of the stages above, under a sand heap.

Head once again into the focal lobby and clear the sand on the ground. Hit the change to lift the door and make a long-lasting easy route. Save at the Bird Statue.

The sand-filled district on the west side of the fundamental corridor appears to be uncrossable, yet a look at the Dungeon Map shows in any case. Follow the light-shaded locales to remain safe. Also, the Chuchus here stay on the protected locales so you can focus on them. You can't, in any case, place markers. Faltering!

A region with a chest is uncovered on your guide toward the west of the main safe spot. Uncover an opening in the divider with your Gust Bellows and slither in. The section ends in a little room with a Chest with a Rare Item

Get back to the sand pit in the focal chamber and proceed with north on the imperceptible walkways set apart on the guide. Enter another opening (check your guide) behind a heap of sand to discover a section prompting a room loaded up with sand heaps.

You realize what to do: Take out the Gust Bellows and clear the room, cautiously staying away from the spikes. A Red Rupee Chest can be found in the northwest corner of the room, a switch is under some sand in the northwest corner that opens the entryway up the steps, and a Pink Fairy in the upper east corner.

Pass through the entryway at the highest point of the steps. Back in the primary chamber, brush some sand off of the mine truck and whack the Timeshift Stone inside the heap of rocks on the actual truck. This will kick it into movement.

A Sentrobe will obstruct your way. Take it out with all around coordinated Shield counters. The Sentrobe Bombs can, obviously, be sliced into equal parts along their creases. In the following stretch of rail, take cover behind the truck to keep away from the Beamos' shafts. One in your way should be chopped down.

At the point when the truck shows up at its objective you can utilize the Gust Bellows to open an entryway to the Bird Statue you recently saved at. Save there and afterward return through the door to investigate the northeastern region.

Another mine truck with a Timeshift Stone can be uncovered in the east. Hit the stone and follow it past the locked entryway to a breeze lock.

Utilize the Gust Bellows to open the breeze lock. At the point when the truck gets to the furthest limit of its track, whack the Stone to turn it off, then, at that point betray again to get the truck to invert so you can get to the entryway.

In the eastern room, cross the transport line cautiously, staying away from the air blasts. Utilize the Slingshot to get adversaries crazy free from plants and climb them.

At the top, throw bombs into the sculptures' crates to get to the heap of sand clouding a Timeshift Stone in the southwest corner. Hit the Stone and cross back toward the east side of the room.

From here you can stumble into the three transport lines. You must time your hurry to stay away from the stones.

Presently, utilize the breeze fueled stage to cross toward the west side of the room. Here you will discover another Sentrobe and a few sculptures with containers you can clear with bombs. Behind these is a piece of information to a riddle across the room.

Move the stage close to you toward the south with the Gust Bellows and get on it. Force it up again to cross toward the north. Make an alternate route by pushing a case down, then, at that point get on another breeze fueled stage along the eastern divider.

There are three sculptures here you can bomb to uncover three switches. You should, nonetheless, hit the switches in a particular request to open the northern entryway. Confronting the pink switches, hit them in a specific order: LEFT, RIGHT, MIDDLE. This relates to the wall paintings across the way.

Enter the open door in the north and two Armos will welcome you. Take on each in turn with the Gust Bellows and sword punches.

With both disposed of you can get to the Chest with the Ancient Circuit (Boss Key) inside. This likewise opens the entryway back to the focal corridor.

To get back to the focal corridor, you can hop off the breeze fueled stage to a western stage beneath.

From here you can get to the top edge on the eastern side of the focal lobby. Up here is a Red Rupee Chest and a case you can push to make an easy route back to southern region.

To cross the gap in the north, hit the Timeshift Stone on the mine truck and bounce on the breeze fueled stage close to the track. Stay simply behind the truck as it changes the region and stop the air fountains. On the far side, save at the Bird Statue.

Approach the Boss Door and addition the Ancient Circuit. Pivot it to frame the state of the lock and the entryway will open.

Thousand-Year Arachnid Moldarach

The Moldarach is perhaps the least demanding supervisor in the game on the off chance that you know what you are doing. The way in to the primary portion of the fight is to consistently step back while locked on to one of the hooks. This will guarantee you will not get it - insofar as you assault the flimsy points when the hooks open.

At the point when a paw opens, cut at it to hit the eye inside. While you step back you can turn your lock-on focuses by tapping the Z button. Utilizing this technique you can quickly focus on the open hook and slice at it, keeping it from assaulting.

Before long one hook will be taken out, then, at that point the other, and Moldarach will change strategies. You can now just harm it by punching its eye.

Sneaking by the sand, the Moldarach will attempt to assault you covertly. You should search for a little knot moving about.

Shower the knot in the sand with the Gust Bellows to uncover the beast. On the off chance that you uncover its body, it will reemerge, permitting you to move in for a quick hit to the eye. Do this a modest bunch of times and you will kill the beast.

Snatch the Heart Container when the room discharges and pass through the entryway. In the Next room, send the Beetle to hit the Timeshift Stone in the overhanging edge, and ride the mine truck as far as possible.

Stop The Imprisoned

Head for Faron Woods subsequent to loading up on Potions and fixing your safeguard in Skyloft. An enormous supervisor fight is simply ahead, so you'll need to be ready.

As you drop into the Woods, Groose will show up behind you, following you underneath the mists. After the cutscene, you can converse with Gorko momentarily about Goddess Walls and Gossip Stones and afterward head for the Sealed Grounds altar.

Converse with the old woman in the altar and she'll show you the methods of the Goddess' Harp. Maybe the main thing to recollect is that 'you don't choose the Harp from the menu screens, you basically press UP to take it out whenever.'

To start with, take out the Goddess' Harp and swing the Wii Remote to and fro, musically, from left to right, coordinating with the pendulum-like movement of the elderly person's hair.

Presently, follow the circle of light in a similar way, coordinating with your left-to-right movements to the extending and contracting of the circle. (Model: As it recoils, move left, and when it develops, swing right). You should remain on schedule, as though you are conduction to the beat given.

In the event that you play the Goddess' Harp effectively during the elderly person's melody, she will complete it and you will become familiar with the Ballad of the Goddess.

There's no an ideal opportunity for playing music, be that as it may, since the cutscene closes with some upheaval outside in the Sealed Grounds.

Leave the hallowed place and hop down the levels of the Sealed Grounds, utilizing the Sail Cloth to break your falls. At the base, The Imprisoned will pop up.

The Imprisoned

In this fight your general objective is to prevent the beast from getting to the highest point of the winding pathway. This is genuinely simple in the event that you realize what you're doing. There are two techniques, the two of which will be depicted underneath. I consider the second simpler.

Method 1 - cut the toes.

The toes can be obliterated with typical sword assaults. It assists with locking on to a toe, and, on the off chance that you have the Stamina, to utilize a Sword Spin assault. This functions admirably on the bunches of toes toward the front.

Start with the back toes, however. When those are gone, the monster will moderate a little. After each toe is eliminated The Imprisoned will step its foot. This is your prompt to deal with the other foot.

When every one of the toes on the two feet are obliterated, the beast will fall on its back. Now you need to get to its head no holds barred - regardless of whether you need to tumble off an edge and utilize a spring or just go around it, arrive quick!

At the point when you get to the head, lock on to the column and swing your sword in an upwards movement to drive it into The Imprisoned's head.

It will then, at that point back up and journey around the fight region, powerful for a couple of seconds. Set aside this effort to cross the region, looking for where it stops.

You presently need to rehash this whole cycle two additional occasions. For the last round, the beast's feet will radiate perilous shockwaves. This essentially implies you need to time your assaults. Go for the back toes first. From that point forward, run a long ways in front of the monster, top off your Stamina Gauge and focus on a foot.

Lock on, move in while the foot is down and utilize a Sword Spin and some essential assaults to take out the toes. You ought to have the option to drop the beast a third time.

Method 2 - time your leaps cautiously.

The technique I found simpler isn't to make a big deal about the toes. Hop/get down to the actual center of the pit, and utilize the immense vent that opened up where the seal used to be. On the off chance that you slant the wii far off you can likely land straight on the imprisoneds head, despite how this might be quicker, however its likewise harder. Its a lot simpler to land one level over the detained, and when he is directly close to you, drop down onto his head and drive the spike in with downwards slices.

Drive the spike into its head a third time and the monster will be sucked into the seal. Approach the seal, raise your blade and play out a Skyward Strike to seal The Imprisoned back in its ethereal confine. To finish the seal, you need to slice your sword in the triangle shape shown. This isn't hard. Simply swing corner to corner down to one side, then, at that point up to one side, and afterward evenly to one side to finish the seal.

Return back to the place of worship and another cutscene will happen where you will be coordinated back to Skyloft.

Leave through the side entryway. Outside, by the Bird Statue behind the sanctum, you can converse with Gorko about Gossip Stones.

At whatever point you see a fix of Blessed Butterflys, you can press UP on the D-cushion and take out the Goddess' Harp in where they assemble and play it a couple of times to call up a Gossip Stone. These stones offer tips, yet they likewise give you a Treasure each time.

While you are here, note that you can get the little birds with your net in the clearing with Gorko for Bird Feathers.

Get back to Skyloft.
The Light Tower

The Light Tower, in the court at the south finish of Skyloft, holds an extraordinary mystery, however it should be actuated by two windmills on one or the other part of town. Prior to meddling with the windmills, converse with Gaepora.

Director Gaepora is on the second floor of the Knight Academy behind some swinging doors at the highest point of the steps. He'll give you the verses to the Ballad of the Goddess, which have an idea in them, alluding to "two spinning sails."

The primary spinning sail is the windmill by the Bazaar on the west part of town. Head over to this and analyze its base. The little Windmill Propeller here can be actuated with your Gust Bellows!

Blow on the Windmill Propeller and the whole windmill will pivot. You should pivot it so it faces the Light Tower. A marker on its base will agree with another marker when it's in position.

The other windmill is a bit more muddled. Approach the windmill on the slope on the far east part of town. As you do, Jakamar will converse with you (he will ONLY show up in the event that you've conversed with Gaepora).

He'll inform you to go see Gondo regarding a robot. Head to the Bazaar and you'll discover Gondo in the Scrap Shop.

Gondo needs a particular Treasure, an Ancient Flower to fix the robot. You ought to have an enormous stock of these from Lanayru Desert, however on the off chance that you don't check the Ancient Flower area for certain areas.

Give him the bloom and he will fix Scrapper, an old robot that can be utilized for various Side Quests. He can likewise be utilized to pull the Windmill Propeller up to the sky. It's fallen underneath to Eldin Volcano.

Travel to the Volcano and land at the Temple Entrance Bird Statue. The Propeller is simply toward the west of the entryway. It's down a sandy slope by the fallen watch tower. You got a Piece of Key here prior.

Scrapper will pull this to the sky, leaving you with nothing else to do except for follow it. Back at Skyloft, a cutscene will play and you would now be able to turn this eastern windmill.

Make it face the Light Tower and the pinnacle will change

Climb the Light Tower and, in the ring at the top, press UP on the D-cushion to pull out the Goddess' Harp. This will enact the pinnacle, permitting you to play the Hymn of the Goddess alongside Fi's beat. By and by, watch the ring grow and agreement and wave the Wii Remote from side-to-favor it.

After you finish the tune, a shaft will open a way into the Thunderhead.

Into The Thunderhead

Your objective in the Thunderhead is the Isle of Storms. This stormy region is actually similar to some other piece of the sky. On the off chance that you have any Goddess Cubes that opened chests here, you would now be able to get them.

Land on the southeastern foundation of the Isle of Songs and you'll be faced with a huge riddle.

The answer for the riddle is to arrange the projecting piece of each ring. You can move the rings with the middle gadget, which you can push in a clockwise way.

A stone with three gems in it to one side of the focal gadget raises little dividers. You can find each ring's projecting fragment on the dividers to stop it and let the others pivot into place close by it.

This takes a bit of experimentation, however the eventual outcome ought to have every one of the little projections arranged in a 12 O'Clock position. They will all turn immediately in the event that you line them up, so dump the entirety of the dividers far removed on the off chance that you get them arranged and move the three projecting sections to the 12 O'Clock position.

Here is a bit by bit answer for the riddle:

Start off by pivoting the middle square clockwise multiple times.

Hit the gem that is on the right side to change which hindrances are up.

Rotate the middle square clockwise multiple times to arrange the squares all in succession.

Hit the top precious stone to change the boundaries.

Rotate the middle square clockwise 1 time.

Hit the precious stone on the right side indeed.

Rotate the squares multiple times to adjust the scaffold appropriately.

NOTE: If you committed an error you can generally bounce onto your Loftwing and essentially jump back onto the Isle of tunes to reset the riddle.

With the extension set up, cross it and creep into the little opening. Inside the structure, utilize a Skyward Strike to enact the wing shape.

You will get familiar with Farore's Courage, a tune you can use in Faron Woods. Presently you can utilize it to get to the Silent Realm in Faron Woods.

The Silent Realm - Faron Woods

Fly back to Faron Woods and land at the Viewing Platform Bird Statue. A shimmering spot only underneath here marks where you can utilize the Goddess' Harp.

This will open the Silent Realm entry. In the Silent Realm you can't utilize any things and the region you can investigate is exceptionally restricted. You will likely fill your Spirit Vessel with Tears found in the Silent Realm. They can be seen better when you get a Light Fruit. This makes a light emission shoot high up over the Tears that you see from a long way away - for 30 seconds. The Light Fruit's belongings don't stack. On the off chance that you get two, the occasions don't make any sense.

The Tears fill a twofold need. They likewise keep the foe Guardians snoozing. One touch from these colleagues and it's Game Over. You'll have to begin the whole minigame once again. Each Tear allows you 90 Seconds of rest from the foes.

You should likewise be careful about Waking Water, the gleaming water that floods certain spaces of the Silent Realm. This awakens the Guardians right away.

Additionally, there are adversaries with lights that will spot you and even seek after you on the off chance that you stroll inside their look. In the event that they ring their chimes, the Guardians will awaken right away.

Snap to amplify map.

There are 15 Tears of Farore to gather in the Silent Realm, and 9 Dusk Relics. Note that you can get endless Dusk Relics here by gathering them, then, at that point getting captured by a Guardian. Your gathered Relics will continue to the following endeavor!

Inside the Great Tree

You can enter the Great Tree from the eastern side of Faron Woods. The pool here has a cavern at the base. Swim through the cavern and you can utilize the air pockets to recuperate your air meter

Surface Inside the Great Tree and move up the plants. You can utilize your Slingshot to take out the Froaks, which should kill the Bokoblin on the stage.

These stages are openly swinging in the breeze, so add a bit of breeze yourself with the Gust Bellows to make them swing. Rather than intersection the region through stages, utilize the first to swing towards the green edge toward the south.

Bounce across and you can follow the stages up a Keese-filled way to a Chest with a Gold Rupee in it. Utilize your Beetle to chop down the Deku Baba.

Take the western exit at the foundation of the tree (you can jump down to this stage from a higher place) and you'll end up on the edge of the tree.

To climb the tree you can utilize the plants, however you'll need to clear the bugs off first. A hornet's home is additionally over the plants, so destroy that and go through your net to clean the hornets that come after you. (Note: If you utilize the Hook Beetle to get the Hornet's home, you can drop the home on the stage you are remaining on to get Hornet Larvae just as gather hornets that come after you with the Bug Net.)

Enter the entryway and you will get yourself vis-à-vis with a Wooden Shield Moblin. This furious monster is a lot simpler to deal with without a safeguard. Despite the fact that you can cut the safeguard to pieces, it's a superior plan to throw a Bomb at the foundation of the safeguard and let it accomplish the work for you.

After this current it's an issue of slicing at the Moblin and impeding it's assaults (ideally with a repulsing safeguard strike).

Exit through the entryway past the Moblin and you'll end up back on the Great Tree's outer stages. Save at the Great Tree Bird Statue. Slice through the crowds of Bokoblins and Keese until you get to the top.

Here you'll track down the dozing Kikwi called Yerbal. Shoot Yerbal with a Slingshot pellet to awaken him. A cutscene will happen. Prior to doing whatever else, you might need to assemble a portion of the space's Goddess Cubes

Northern Goddess Cube

Hop off a stage high up on the north side of the Great Tree to arrive on the stage close to the ground beneath with a rope prompting the Goddess Cube.

You should stamp the stage early with a waypoint on your guide so you can bounce down to it without any problem.

This opens a chest with a Rupee Medal inside on an island in the northern piece of the Thunderhead.

Note: An Evil Crystal can be found in a Chest on this island.

Southwest Goddess Cube

Hop off a stage high up on the southwest side of the Great Tree to arrive on a stage on one of the roots on the western side.

This opens a chest on the west side of Skyloft with a Silver Rupee in it. You can run off the wooden stage and control your tumble to arrive at the gliding island with the chest.

Since you can swim with the Water Dragon's Scale you should get back to Skyloft and gather the Heart Piece in the Goddess Chest in the focal point of town. You need to swim to arrive. A Sliver Rupee Chest is close to it.

Lake Floria

The passageway to Lake Floria is at the far southern finish of Faron Woods. To open it you need to bring a Skyward Strike up before it and afterward draw a circle where one is absent. This total plan can be found by the Viewing Platform on the ground in the far north in the event that you need a reference.

You can gather a Red Rupee prior to plunging into the lake far underneath.

Give the current drag you access to the caverns of Lake Floria. Here you will meet a red Parella who at first escapes from you, however at that point helps you out. As you seek after it, it will withdraw behind certain sheets. You can without much of a stretch break these with a twist assault (shake the nunchuk). The Parella will then, at that point lead you through the passages.

The following region is loaded up with Froaks. These dangerous creatures of land and water can be utilized to clear the many stone dividers nearby for Rupees, including two Red Rupees behind the northwest stone divider and a Silver Rupee under the broke stone in the actual focal point of the space. To point your assaults at the Froaks all the more effectively, lock onto them.

However long you are locked on and the Froak is among you and the broke item, it will turn into it and explode.

Save at the Bird Statue. The main divider to break is in the northwest. This will permit you to proceed.

Before long you'll need to utilize a twist assault to clear a door. Point up at the door from underneath, twist and you can bounce directly over it like an obstacle.

The following chamber has a Chest with a Goddess Plume inside. You'll need to surface and search for it on the dry ground.

Lake Floria Goddess Cube

In a chamber under Lake Floria you can discover a Goddess Cube on a segment of dry land. It's in a chamber with a Bird Statue and a chest with a Goddess Plume inside. You need the Clawshots to get to the chest on the east side of Skyloft.

Hop over another door and you'll track down a goliath adversary fish in your way. This is extremely simple to kill. Utilize a twist assault on it to stagger it, then, at that point lock on and turn ideal for its goliath brow to take it out.

On the edges over this pool you can score a Pink Fairy in the skulls.

The entryway on the north side of this room must be opened by your Parella companion. The Water Dragon is on the opposite side.

Converse with the Water Dragon, Faron and she'll request a jug of Sacred Water. You would now be able to utilize your Dowsing capacity to track down the Sacred Water, which is in the Skyview Temple, everything being equal.

A Chest on one side of this chamber contains an Evil Crystal and another Chest contains a Silver Rupee, so don't miss those.

Utilize the way to leave the submarine caverns and save at the Bird Statue. In the event that you remain at the Bird Statue and send your Beetle up high and toward the west you can utilize it to gather a Gold Rupee! You might see the Goddess Cube here, yet you can't arrive at it until you get the Clawshots.

At long last, a Gossip Stone can be raised here for a sign about a Goddess Wall and a Monster Claw.

Skyview Temple

At the point when you take the way driving back to Faron Woods you can make an easy route back to the lake by pushing the log off of the edge.

You should now get back to Skyview Temple. You can enter the Sky through a Bird Statue and afterward land down at the Temple. You need an Empty Bottle for this next region, so make certain to have one around (or one you can purge in a little).

Enter Skyview Temple and head down the steps until you go to a bunch of Blessed Butterflys. You can play the Goddess' Harp here to make a Goddess Wall show up.

Your Mogma mate Ledd will likewise show up here. He's investigating the region for Treasure. As you advance toward the overwhelmed chamber, you'll find a recently locked entryway.

To track down the Small Key, take the northeastern entryway and bounce into the overflowed eastern room. Swim to the base and through the little passage. On the opposite side, climb the plants to discover the burrow spot with the Small Key in it.

Be careful with the Green Bokoblins with bolts. You can hinder their bolts however in the event that you don't time it right your safeguard's solidarity can be sapped rapidly. It's ideal to be forceful: Just run at them and thump them into the water.

A Staldra currently watches the room just beyong the locked entryways. You can kill these effectively with a Bomb. Take the northern entryway.

Two Bokoblins with bows and bolts are guarding the tight rope. Taking cover behind a mushroom will impede the bolts, yet you are still allowed to use your Hook Beetle. Note that a Bomb Plant has developed over the space, so you can utilize the Hook Beetle to convey a bomb squarely into their revolting appearances.

Save at the Bird Statue. In the supervisor room are three Stalfos. You can utilize similar strategies from previously (coordinated obstructing and utilizing the Wiimotion to put your cut where their blades aren't) to dispose of them, however note that bombs will likewise make them shed their appendages.

In the wake of killing the Stalfos you can enter the spring behind the manager room and Dowse for the Sacred Water. The Pink Fairy crowd parts with the cascade with the Sacred Water. Remain here and utilize your Empty Bottle to grab some water up.

You will be gotten back to the sanctuary entrance in the wake of getting the Sacred Water. Fly into the sky and afterward land at the Floria Waterfall Bird Statue. Go through the way to get back to the Water Dragon's area.

Approach the Dragon and she will make the way for the Ancient Cistern (Dungeon 4) in a cutscene. It's behind Floria Waterfall. Save at the Bird Statue and, in case you are exceptional for a prison, head in.

Antiquated Cistern

After entering the Ancient Cistern you will end up in an overflowed room with a monster sculpture. The sculpture's lowered hands each hold a Silver Rupee. To get the Silver Rupee in each hand, you need to swim straight up to the edge of the hand and afterward play out a Spin by shaking the Nunchuck to rapidly get the Rupee before the hand closes. In case you are gotten, shake the Wii Remote to get free.

Since you are 200 Rupees more extravagant, approach the locked entryway at the focal point of the sculpture. You'll require a Small Key to get inside, however until further notice you can peruse the tablet to one side of it. This tablet provides you a particular insight into a close by entryway, it makes an interpretation of, generally, to TOP, BOTTOM, LEFT, RIGHT.

Enter the entryway on the east side of the primary chamber. A change to one side of the entryway opens it. Dip under swim to the surface. Note that the cushions in the water will flip in the event that you drop from a huge tallness - this will prove to be useful for puzzle tackling later. Be careful with the flipped cushions, notwithstanding, the spikes will hurt you.

The water spout will allow you to leave this room, however proceed toward the north towards the Skulltulas for the present. These Skulltulas are sticking around for their chance in their networks, yet you can cut at the strands a bit to spur them to the ground. At the point when they arrive at the ground, slice at them with an upwards movement to flip them on their back, then, at that point utilize a Fatal Blow to kill them.

The entryway not far off holds an uncommon lock that the tablet in the primary room can help you open. Hit the tabs on the lock with your sword in a specific order: Top tab, Bottom tab, Left tab, Right tab.

In the following room you'll discover more lotus leaf root cushions, however the genuine danger is on the roof above. The Skulltulas here will possibly drop on the off chance that you get close to them. Leave the lotus leaf pull cushions and hang tight for one to drop. Whack it to the side to make it twist and afterward wound its stomach twice. You can likewise cut their web with the Beetle to make them fall into the water.

Shoot the Walltula with your Slingshot and afterward climb the plants in the southeast corner. From here you can hop onto the lotus leaf root cushion along the eastern divider to flip it over and open the lowered section driving east and afterward south.

You can't get the Red Rupee in this room, so take the entry to the following room. Twist through the sheets and, on the far side, open the entryway. You'll wind up at the chest with the Small Key.

Get back to the focal chamber. Save at the Bird Statue by the passage. Open the locked entryway on the sculpture's base in the focal region. Inside you can do close to nothing however drop to the ground floor. Here you'll experience the Stalmaster miniboss.

Stalmaster Miniboss

Stalmaster gets going the battle with two arms welding blades in each hand. as the fight advances it will wind up with four arms, three blades and one fight hatchet. To prevail in

the battle against Stalmaster you'll need to assault any region it isn't guarding, additionally be careful with its wild assaults and to avoid the numerous approaching hacks and cuts of its various arms.

Maybe the best system is to utilize safeguard counter assaults to make it drop the entirety of its arms. At the point when you do this, circle back to a Spin Attack yet be prepared to counter once more! Watch your safeguard wellbeing also, since this amazing adversary will decimate your Shields.

There are Hearts in the skulls along the edge of the room. After the Stalmaster is crushed an entryway will open and a chest here contains the prison's most prominent fortune: The Whip!

You can utilize the Whip to enact the switches inside the sculpture. Every one will enact a spout of water. Lock on with the Whip and utilize the springs to advance up.

Head once again into the primary chamber (the top region with the Boss Key Lock is difficult to reach). You can utilize the steps on the east side of the space to get up to the Chest along the north mass of the fundamental chamber.

You'll need to swing across the whip grasp point that juts from the divider. Lock on to the whip grasp and you can swing across. Here you'll discover the Dungeon Map.

Dip under the guide and climb onto the lotus leaf root cushions on the north side of the pool. From here you ought to have the option to see a divider switch. You can enact this with the Whip, yet you need to get close to it first.

Utilize the Whip to lock on to the closest lotus leaf root cushion and flip it. This will point the spikes descending and a protected cushion will surface. Step onto it, lock on to the divider switch and yank it with the Whip.

You would now be able to swim into the opening underneath the water on the west side of the room. Follow it to the following chamber and open the Red Rupee Chest behind the pool where you surface. Kill the Skulltula.

In this room there is a switch behind an entryway. You can get this divider switch with your Whip and initiate it THROUGH the bars. Lock on first to make this simpler.

There is a Goddess Wall in this room, and a few adversaries - Green Bokoblins, Deku Babas, Chuchus and Walltulas; nothing you haven't seen previously. The Goddess Wall is on the southern side of the room.

Your objective is the turning column up the steps. Climb this and ride it around to the far stage. From here, search for a whip hold. Join your Whip to it and hold down on the Analog Stick to stop swinging. Turn towards the switch and afterward shake the Wii Remote to swing towards it.

Delivery your swing and get the divider switch. You would now be able to get back to the whip grasp and swing to the plants under the now-open mesh.

Enact the switch with your Whip and a whirlpool will open in the focal point of the room. Make a plunge.

You will surface in a room with Skulltulas on the roof. Get on dry ground and get the Amber Relic. Send your Beetle out to chop the Skulltulas down. One falling Skulltula will flip the lotus leaf root cushion and permit you to swim under it into the following region.

There is a green Bokoblin sitting on the opposite side of the bars here with a Small Key on its belt. Lock onto the adversary and utilize the Whip to yank the Key off of its belt. You would then be able to utilize it to open the close by locked entryway.

On the opposite side you'll see a short cutscene uncovering the locaiton of the Boss Key Chest. After this, kill the Bokoblin and bounce into the flood of water.

In the following room you can move up onto a stage and pull a divider change to open the door. Hit the close by Walltula with the Beetle. Bounce into the water and utilize a twist move to hop onto the shore on the east side of the room. Get the Amber Relic in the grass and afterward utilize the Whip to pivot the close by lotus leaf root cushion.

You would now be able to get on the gliding cushion and climb the plants. Hop off the edge in the actual focus of the room and you can flip the lotus leaf root cushion, uncovering an entry underneath the water.

Swim through this entry and gather the Red Rupee. Twist through the Froaks and surface to discover a switch you can enact with the Whip.

This raises the lotus leaf root cushion you just flipped onto a fountain. Get back to it in the focal point of the room and flip it on the spring with your whip. Cross the cushion toward the western side of the room.

Utilize your Whip to pull the divider switch and get back to the focal room. The Furnix that welcomes you here can be killed with the Whip.

Delay until it spreads out its padded tail and hit it with the Whip. Yank the tail towards you and it will tumble to the ground. Polish it off with a Fatal Blow.

A Red Rupee chest is underneath the stage. You can move down to it utilizing the plants. Utilizing the plants you can likewise move to a close by stage almost an enormous switch. Yanking this switch with the Whip will make the huge focal sculpture slip, similar to a monster lift.

You would now be able to enter the sculpture and drop to the base. Utilize the base entryway in the sculpture to get to another underground region.

Here you'll discover Cursed Bokoblins, which drop the very uncommon Evil Crystal arbitrarily. They are scared of the Sacred Shield and its redesigns, so hold that out before you and they will not screw with you.

To kill a Cursed Bokoblin, you need to hit it with a Spin Attack to flip it on its back. When it's on the ground, utilize a Fatal Blow to polish it off.

There is a reviled pool in this space you ought to totally keep away from, however above it are a couple of gleaming blue eyes cut into the stone that you can send your Beetle through for Rupees and Hearts.

Head northwest and hack up some more Cursed Bokoblins. Leave onto the lotus leaf root cushions in the water and flip one of them with the Whip. Remain here and shoot your Beetle through the arrangement of eyes ignoring the pool and you can hit a pink switch.

This stops the cascade nearby, making a way for your Beetle to convey a Bomb to a broke column (then again you can confront the Bomb with your back to the cascade then, at that point discharge your Beetle to convey the Bomb round the alternate way). Head for the rear of the cascade and kill the Fire Keese. Utilize the Beetle to convey a Bomb to the broke stone in the gap and you will actually want to utilize the Whip to swing across it.

Climb the primary plant column on the opposite side to the exceptionally top. Hop from here to the following one and ride it around to the far side.

Run down the incline and bounce across to the plant divider, at the highest point of which you can get to a switch. Utilizing the Whip, toss this switch to one side to invert the turn of the numerous columns nearby, and the plate of stone beneath. Bounce down to this plate and proceed up the slope, killing the Bokoblins in your way.

You can ride another column around to get to the opposite side of a similar switch you just whipped. Invert the switch again and head back to the column you just rode. It's presently turning the alternate way. Ride it to another space.

In this pit loaded up with bones a rope prompts the surface. Prior to climbing it, enact the switch in the following room with your Whip to cause a spring to show up for an alternate route back to the underlying underground region.

Presently, climb the rope. As you do, many Cursed Bokoblins will pursue you, infrequently getting you. Shake the Bokoblins off by shaking the Wii Remote and Nunchuk.

At the top you'll wind up back in the primary Ancient Cistern chamber. Pull the divider switch and you can get to the switch that actuates the sculpture's development.

Flip this switch to raise the sculpture, consequently uncovering the Boss Key Chest beneath!

Plunge down the opening with the rope. Head for the fountain and you'll discover the sculpture has lifted past it and the Chest is available to anyone. Open it to track down the Blessed Idol (Boss Key).

Presently, the sculpture will come smashing down and Bokoblins will trap you. Disregard them and run for the edge. This sculpture can kill you immediately, so be careful!

At the point when the sculpture arrives set up, enter the entryway at its base and take the springs up. Save in the primary chamber and afterward head for the locked supervisor entryway at the highest point of the sculpture.

Spot the Blessed Idol in the keyhole, confronting the small sculpture inwards and afterward pivoting it to the right position. This opens the obstruction to the rooftop.

Head up the steps and Whip each of the four changes to raise the gigantic sculpture. Save at the Bird Statue at the top and ensure you are ready for an extreme manager fight prior to going up the steps.

Antiquated Automaton Koloktos

This fight has two separate stages. The first has it immovably established in the focal point of the room. You can stay away from the tossed cutting edges by side-hopping (lock on, press to one side or right and press A).

In spite of the fact that you might need to stay away, it's smarter to get in near insult the Koloktos.

Doing as such will actuate an assault where it crushes the ground.

On the off chance that you get right up front and Koloktos hits the ground, avoid its arm and afterward utilize the Whip to hook onto its arm and pull it off. Do this a subsequent time and the beast will change its technique, then again tossing cutting edges and, in the event that you draw near, swiping at you.

Now, its gleaming red flimsy spot is uncovered and you should get in to assault it with your sword. Do this by expecting its moves and conceivably countering its swiped with your Shield.

After it takes some harm it reconstructs. You'll have to do this whole standard a second time now. When you harm its center more, it will change to its subsequent stage.

In this stage the Koloktos will start moving about the room. Note that it can thump down the segments nearby to uncover Hearts or you can utilize one of his sabers (see underneath on the most proficient method to acquire) to thump down the segment to a similar end.

The Koloktos will presently generate Cursed Bokoblins on the off chance that you move excessively far away, so maintain at a medium separation and evade its assaults until it pounds the ground. This time you can rip three arms off as they hit the ground at the same time.

At the point when they do, they will leave behind a goliath saber for each arm. You can pick these up and use them. You can just perform, moderate, intentional assaults with the monster saber, so prepare.

You don't have to rip off the other three arms. All things considered, run for Koloktos' base and play out an even swipe with the goliath saber to remove its legs.

Presently, assault its center more than once from a slight distance to break the mesh and harm the red flimsy part with your enormous saber.

You need to pull off this normal twice more to completely drain the adversary's life.

Get back to Skyloft

After the fight, gather your Heart Container and enter the entryway. On the opposite side, utilize a Skyward Strike to hit the wing token.

The blazes of Farore will charge your blade, giving it twice the killing force!

Return the Isle of Storms in the Thunderhead. Enter the structure and Skyward Strike the winged symbol to start a cutscene. You will gain proficiency with Nayru's Wisdom, which will open the Silent Realm - Lanayru Desert.

The Silent Realm - Lanayru Desert

At the point when you initial jump into Lanayru Desert, select the North Desert Bird Statue. That way, you will be close to the spot to begin the

Silent Realm. Utilize your Dowsing capacity to detect the shine region close by (with the Goddess Butterflies zooming around it). Once there, pull out your harp and play it in a state of harmony with the ring all together for the Silent Realm marker to show up. Go to the marker and push your sword into the ground to start the Silent Realm.

This Silent Realm assortment binge is similar as the final remaining one. There are 15 Tears to gather and 7 Dusk Relic areas. You can replay this level and the Dusk Relics will move around, yet respawn in the areas beneath.

Snap for a bigger guide.

In this Silent Realm you actually need to stay away from the sand trap. It's ideal to leave some simple Tears on the focal stage so you can run for them on the off chance that you need them.

Recollect that your guide is as yet helpful to show the areas of lowered dividers. Here are some interesting Tears:

In the south region, a Tear on a confine expects you to move a mine truck.

Another Tear is skimming noticeable all around in the south. Move a mine truck under it when the water subsides.

One Tear is in a tree in the far south. Roll into the tree to cut it down.

One Tear is in the desert sands toward the north. Utilize the guide to discover the balance to get to it.

One Tear in the north is on a divider protected by adversaries with lights. Stay away from the first by remaining aside while it passes. You can alert the following one since you are directly close to the Tear and you can snatch it to quiet it down.

For finishing the Silent Realm you will get an astounding award: the Clawshots!

You can utilize the Clawshots to hook onto any objective OR plants. Give it a shot here in the desert to totally stay away from the sand trap. There are a few Chests, Goddess Cubes and Heart Pieces you would now be able to reach.

Since you have the Clawshots you can get some extraordinary stuff nearby and then some.

Open the Chest on the stage close to the Silent Realm entrance. Inside is a Dusk Relic.

Get Heart Piece 19

Get two Lanayru Desert Goddess Cubes, 22 and 23 (Heart Medal and Life Medal)

Open Goddess Cube Chest 8 (Skyloft, Gold Rupee)

Get the Goddess Cubes in Faron Woods and Deep Woods, 5 and 6 (Heart Piece and Rupee Medal).

Head toward the West Desert Bird Statue. A question mark denotes the sand cascade in the southwest of Lanayru Desert. You would now be able to utilize the Clawshots to arrive at a cavern entrance in the cascade.

Lanayru Caves

In the minuscule Lanayru Caves region, approach Golo, a Goron working on a divider in the south. Golo will give you a Small Key that permits you to enter the Sand Sea toward the west.

Prior to leaving the cavern, open the close by Chest for a Monster Horn. Use theeastern exit from the cavern to arrive at the underlying Lanayru Mine region. Utilizing the Clawshots, you can get another TreasureChest with an Evil Crystal inside.

Head back to the Lanayru Caves and utilize Small Key on the western way to enter the Sand Sea area.

Sand Sea

Head toward the West Desert Bird Statue. A question mark denotes the sand cascade in the southwest of Lanayru Desert. You would now be able to utilize the Clawshots to arrive at a cavern entrance in the cascade.

Lanayru Caves

In the minuscule Lanayru Caves region, approach Golo, a Goron working on a divider in the south. Golo will give you a Small Key that permits you to enter the Sand Sea toward the west.

Note: If you address Golo by and by, you will get a subsequent Small Key . This Small Key will prove to be useful when you travel to Lanayru Gorge later in the game.

Prior to leaving the cavern, open the close by Chest for a Monster Horn. Utilize the EASTERN exit from the cavern to arrive at the underlying Lanayru Mine region with your Clawshots.

Here you can get another TreasureChest with an Evil Crystal inside.

Head back to the Lanayru Caves and utilize Small Key on the western way to enter the Sand Sea area.

Sand Sea

In the Sand Sea, your first thing to take care of is getting across a huge gap. Utilize the Clawshots to move from one objective to another.

Sand Sea Goddess Cube

A Goddess Cube can be found just toward the north of the harbor at the passageway to the Sand Sea. Move up the payload compartments and utilize the Clawshots to catch onto the objective in the far north. Drop down to discover a room loaded with Arachas and a Goddess Cube in the corner. This opens a chest in the Bazaar in Skyloft with a Gold Rupee in it!

Presently, head to the dock in the west focal area. Here you'll discover a boat moored with a Timeshift Stone on it. Initiate the stone.

Converse with the resuscitated LD-301N Skipper robot on the dock and he'll offer to take you to the Skipper's Retreat, set apart on your guide with a X in the far south.

Get on the boat and you'll have the option to investigate the Sand Sea. Actually,"Explore" isn't by and large the right word, since you can't do everything except go to the Skipper's Retreat moor and get off the boat.

Note that you can hold A to speed up, and the boat has its own Stamina Meter.

Captain's Retreat

Dock at the Skipper's Retreat and save at the Bird Statue. Advance around the stages, essentially running past the Electro Spumes or throwing bombs at them.

Utilize your Clawshots to start climbing the numerous stages. The drifting Peahats can be utilized as hook focuses. You can make out a Chest on a stage you leave in transit behind, yet you can't get this until you get to the actual top of the Retreat.

On one stage you'll discover a Bomb Plant on a desert plant and a fell divider. Utilize your Beetle to convey the bomb into the divider to make an entry up - that is loaded up with Chuchus. Bomb them from a good ways!

The Metal Shield Moblin on the extension can't be effortlessly assaulted from the front. All things being equal, run towards its safeguard and you can ascend and over it, arriving behind it.

Assault the Metal Shield Moblin from the back to kill it while it's confounded. Get the Red Rupee from the chest on the following stage and kill the Quadro-Baba.

Captain's Retreat Goddess Cube

As you climb the stages in the Skipper's Retreat, you will go to a Metal Shield Moblin on a scaffold. Simply past this is a stage that you can remain on to shoot some dry plants on a verdant tower with your Clawshots. From the plants on the divider, enact your Clawshots and you can arrive at the stage with the Goddess Cube. This opens a chest in the sky on an island to the furthest west of Skyloft. This island has a few chests on it, however this one is in a correctional facility. You need to utilize the Clawshots on the roof of the cell to arrive at the chest, which holds the Potion Medal. This broadens your mixture's belongings.

Hook up to the following stage and you'll need to battle off a Furnix. Utilize the Whip to yank its tail and afterward kill it with a Fatal Blow. Utilize the Whip again to yank the Peahat sprout and the Peahat will start flying towards the following island.

Take hold of the Peahat with the Clawshots and use it to get to the following objective. On this stage, prior to moving to the following objective, utilize your Beetle to chop the Deku Baba down hanging over the objective.
Simply over this objective is a stage with a circle of prickly plants you can backtrack to once you pass it. Open the Chest among the desert

flora for a Monster Horn.

the following pair of Peahats goes all over on one or the other side of a stone arrangement. You should utilize the Clawshots with coordinated accuracy to move from one to the next.

When you get to the top stage you ought to investigate the summit of the Skipper's Retreat for a couple of Sand Cicadas.

Inside the Skipper's Retreat you'll discover a great deal of sand. Pull out your Gust Bellows and get everything out. Under the sand you'll discover Arachas, Rupees and Amber Relics.

On the off chance that you sit on the stool you can recuperate your life and get a clue about the Sand Cicadas from Fi. Underneath the sand is a Chest with the object of your trip: theAncient Sea Chart!

Rather than bringing the zipline down, jump off of the stage utilizing the projecting segment on the west side. You will enter a controllable jump - focus on the little stage with the Chest far underneath. Inside is a Silver Rupee, sweet!

From here you can without much of a stretch utilize the Clawshots to arrive at the Skipper. The Skipper will refresh your guide and point out an area in the far west. Pilot your boat west to the Shipyard entrance.

You might need to utilize your cannon to get out Bokoblins and Electro Spumes en route.

Shipyard

The Shipyard primarily comprises of a mine truck minigame and a (recognizable) manager battle. In the first place, be that as it may, you should manage two Lizalfos (when the shipyard has been finished you can get limitless reptile tails from the two Lizalfos by going all through the Rickety Coaster building). Your new, more impressive sword will slice through them substantially more rapidly. A Shield Bash assault can set the Lizalfo faltering.

Converse with Gortram the Goron inside the structure (you can return here later to play the Rickety Coaster game for a Heart Piece) and jump in the mine truck when you are all set.

Here are some broad tips for the mine truck ride:

The mine truck is constrained by shifting the Wii distant left and right. have a go at holding it with two hands and try to watch Link intently as his body will move noticeably with your shifting.

Tilt towards within each turn. This will speed up (you can back off with B), yet it will likewise keep you adhered to the track like paste.

You can pick a way at crossroads by shifting toward the path you pick. A few ways lead to impasses or endless circles. Study the course map assuming you need to turn into a genius!

Flick the Wii Remote up when you get air off a leap to securely land. Attempt to have a great deal of speed going into a leap.

The subsequent mine truck track has a couple of impasses and a seize the start and two toward the end. You'll presumably have to play this course a couple of times to get its hang, however go ahead and look at the video walkthrough to assist with figuring out how to move.

Save at the Bird Statue on the opposite side of the subsequent mine truck track. Past it is a gigantic pit of sand. In case you are low on hearts, pull up a chair on the stools in the save room prior to continuing!

Head toward the south finish of this pit and utilize the Gust Bellows to clean up the sand. You should uncover another Moldarach. This time you have an all the more impressive sword, so the battle is a bit more limited.

See: Moldarach for supervisor battle subtleties

Step outside after you rout Moldarach and get back to Skipper. He'll guide you to the Pirate Stronghold - a debt of gratitude is in order in vain, Skip!

Privateer Stronghold

At the point when you show up at the Pirate Stronghold you'll observe to be minimal in excess of a Keese-invaded stage. Despite the fact that in the event that you look into just subsequent to getting off the boat, you'll see a couple of openings on the facade of the Stronghold. Send your Beetle in to gather three silver rupees. Subsequent to getting those 300 rupees in your wallet, enter the entryway on the north side to get to the Stronghold inside.

Inside you'll discover a platform that is intended to hold a Timeshift Orb. This is similar as a Timeshift Stone, yet you can convey it. Shockingly, it's no place in sight.

Head down the dusty passage, showering your Gust Bellows on heaps of sand to uncover Red Rupees. Two Lizalfos block your way (the Lizalfos will give reptile tails and you can get limitless reptile tails by over and over leaving all through the privateer fortification, yet not until in the wake of finishing the privateer fortress), and a Spume too. You can run past the Spume to arrive at the most distant side of the sand pit.

Past the entryway is the Timeshift Orb in the northwestern tip of the Pirate Stronghold map. When you start conveying it, all way of antiquated beasts wake up. In the following room, Tecnoblins will impede you.

Use Shield Bashes to counter their assaults and afterward hit them a couple of times with your fueled up blade. Head further south and Beamos will spring to life. Pare them down as you did in Lanayru Mining Facility.

A chest behind a fence must be opened in the event that you ditch your Timeshift Orb at a protected separation from it. The Timeshift Orb opens the fenced-off entryways, yet it will bring hindrances up before numerous others. Inside the Chest is a Silver Rupee.

In the huge, sandy chamber you come to next are two of the uncommon Ancient Flowers you need for the Upgrade System, so don't miss them.

You can utilize the incline in the south finish of this space to get to a progression of stages that raise as you close to them with the Orb. Hop starting with one then onto the next to cross to the entryway in the north.

In the following region, leave the Timeshift Orb by the banished entryway. Its belongings will bring through the way to the far side. Go around here to discover a divider switch that will allow you to recover the Orb

In the following sandy room, leave your Timeshift Orb a bit away from the Chest so it doesn't bring the stage up before it. Cross the sand trap to arrive at the Evil Crystal in the Chest.

Presently, either keep away from or kill the numerous Deku-Babas in the room. Make sure to Shield Bash Babas to make them simpler to slash down.

The following enormous room has a few locked entryways, an Electro Spume and a lot of Technoblins. Your objective here is to leave the Orb by the entryway so you can enter the little chamber and push the box inside onto a switch. This will close the close by door, yet open another. You would now be able to stumble into the sinking sand and enter the way toward the south, with Timeshift Orb close by.

In the wake of getting out the Beamos in the following region, you might see that the region between the four associated rooms has a few bars that will permit the Timeshift Orb's belongings to spread all through the focal region.

Set the Orb in the room by the bars and you would then be able to go around to a divider switch in the bigger space toward the west. A Chest in one of the rooms holds a Monster Horn.

Before you can help the Timeshift sphere through the following arrangement of ways toward the south, you'll need to obliterate two Armos sculptures. Prepare your Gust Bellows and obliterate their precious stones each in turn, tricking them to the edge of the Timeshift Orb impact region to remain in security.

The platform for the Timeshift Orb is simply on the opposite side. Putting the Orb on the platform opens the goliath jaws outside. Head out through the new entryway.

Privateer's Fortress Goddess Cube

At the Pirate Hideout, after you utilize the Timeshift Sphere to open the goliath mouth on the island, you'll leave the inside through an entryway in the focal point of the island.

Look over this entryway for a Clawshots target. Utilize this and another objective to get to the Goddess Cube. This opens a chest on the east side of Skyloft with a Heart Piece inside! Utilize the Clawshots to climb the plant covered islands to the wellspring of the cascade on a coasting island over the town lake.

You should get back to the Skipper again and afterward return to the remnants of the boat by the entryway you just emerged from. Here, Fi will get in touch with you and update your Dowsing capacity to assist with tracking down the missing boat. Which is undetectable!

Get back on the boat and head for the new blemish on your guide, a circle of stones in the upper east space of the ocean.
Sandship

To discover the Sandship you need to venture out toward the upper east space of the Sand Sea and flip on your Dowsing capacity. You can Dowse from the boat and pilot it while you point the cursor.

At the point when you Dowse you will track down a moving, imperceptible mass, gliding in a wide circle around the stones in a ring here. To uncover the boat, seek after it with your Dowsing actuated until you trust you are close.

At the point when you draw near, fire your cannon directly at it (reach skyward) and you should hit it and make it briefly noticeable!

After this, get back to Dowsing and seek after it once more. Fire again to uncover the boat - you'll need to hit it a couple of more occasions to make it totally apparent. At the point when you do as such, Link will move on board in a cutscene.

Floor 1F

Enter the swinging doors on the boat's deck - you can't do whatever else now.

Floor B1

Head down the steps and save at the Bird Statue. There is a Goddess Wall you can actuate here, yet you can't do much else since one foyer prompts an impasse. The other lobby in the south has an entryway and a couple of Keese in it. Enter the entryway here.

Roll a Bomb at the Electro Spume. You can cross the sand trap here, yet you'll have to save your Stamina. Substitute running and strolling and you can arrive at the lobby on the far side.

Head east and enter the entryway at the lower part of the steps.

Floor B2

An Aracha-rounded corridor can be cleared out with a bit of swordplay or the whip. Toward the west is a Boss Door and a Treasure Room, neither of which is available as of now. Enter the entryways in the northern lobby.

In this sand-occupied room you'll track down an unusual entryway lock that requires a particular mix that you enter with blade strikes. The mix turns out to be: BOTTOM, TOP, BOTTOM, RIGHT, and here's the manner by which you sort that out:

Under the sand are four boat wheels with a blue blemish on each, addressing the lock on the entryway. The red paint addresses the TOP of the wheel, so you need to see them according to the right point of view. Also, each wheel has a specific number of red "spokes" showing the request, from one to four.

Notwithstanding, the blend above will open the entryway. Lock on and hit the blue lock parts in the right request. Inside the room you'll track down a Small Key.

Floor 1F

This Small Key opens an entryway on 1F, only opposite the entryway driving out to the deck. Enter this way to battle a miniboss.

LD-002S Scervo

The Scervo robot is obliged to one way, so wounding movements and vertical Spin Attacks work best. All things considered, this quarrel is all over Shield Bash counterattacks.

At the point when you counter Scervo's moves, you can get in a significant number assaults. Each assault pushes Scervo towards an edge somewhere out there, so stay in all out attack mode and possibly hold on to counter on the off chance that it ends up to strike.

On the off chance that you continue to cut Scervo you can get him to the edge and he'll bring a spiked entryway behind you closer. Run straight for him to make up some space and get back to similar strategies.

When you get Scervo to the edge of the boat stage a subsequent time, his blade will tumble off and he'll start utilizing a turning snare assault. This assault is a bit difficult to counter, however you can do it - change to a more guarded procedure and Shield Bash these assaults. Get Scervo to the edge of the stage to win the fight.

For beating Scervo you'll get the Bow. This phenomenal weapon can kill foes from a huge span and initiate Eye Switches all through the Sandship. You can charge an Arrow for your Bow prior to shooting it to make it all the more impressive. It will likewise fly further.

One of these Eye Switches is on the pole shaft of the Sandship. Head to the deck and search for it over the focal point of the boat.

Shoot the Eye Switch to open a Timeshift Stone high above. Hit the Switch and afterward the Stone with your new Bow to change the whole boat.

A Bokoblin will then close the Timeshift Stone's enclosure. This Timeshift Stone is the just one on the whole boat, so your solitary choice is to get up there and open it once more! Ascend the tall stepping stool on the pole post and you will wind up on an unstable bar over the boat.

Utilize your Bow to kill each adversary on the upper poles. An Eye Switch over one of the ziplines can be shot to bring the handle down to you. Utilize this to arrive at the pole toward the west.

Indeed, utilize your Bow to get out each Bokoblin you can see. On the off chance that you shoot them with your Bow, they will drop bolts!

Another Eye Switch/zipline contraption will get you to the far east pole. From here you can open the Timeshift Stone door (however don't deactivate the Stone).

Take the zipline to the short pole in the east and dip under toward the eastern deck.

Heart Piece

When you clear your path through the crow's homes of the Sandship you'll approach the back of the boat. You can utilize the Clawshots to arrive at a Clawshot Target that allows you to drop down the posterior of the boat. A Chest here contains the Heart Piece.

A Goddess Wall can likewise be found on the lower eastern deck. Draw a bolt on this to get more bolts! (It should have a straightforward quill toward one side and a point at the other).

Get back to the primary deck however, before you head back inside the boat, search for an Eye Switch on the raft on the north side of the boat. You need to ascend a stepping stool to get to it.

Floor B1

Head down to B1 and go into the room with the daylight spilling into it along the western divider - by the sand trap pit. You can shoot the Timeshift Stone on the boat's pole through the mesh the light is spilling through to incapacitate it.

Whenever it is handicapped you can go into the adjoining room and open the Chest for the Dungeon Map. Pull the divider switch here to make a way out, and hit the Timeshift Stone again through the mesh in the roof.

Across the sand pit is a foyer with four entryways. On the north and south sides of this foyer are two switches that enact the boat's motor.

Enter the open northeastern entryway first. Kill the Technoblins and afterward move the square onto the floor switch.

This opens the windows of the boat permitting you to complete a few things: You would now be able to utilize the raft you brought from above down to get back to the deck (shoot the Eye Switch on it to drop it up or down, in the event that you neglected to drop it down, get back to the upper deck and shoot it); you can likewise arrive at the generator room far beneath. Yet, you can't do anything in the motor room until you get the parts rolling inside it.

Take the raft up to the deck above and shoot the Timeshift Stone to incapacitate it. Bring the raft down and go into the adjoining room that was recently closed off by power.

In this room is a mesh on the roof. Initiate the Timeshift Stone again through the mesh utilizing your Bow. You can discover a sword space on a contraption toward the side of this room.

Wound it and contort the dial to actuate the moving cylinders underneath in the motor room. you can't, nonetheless, navigate the entire room yet.

Pull the divider change to make the way for the foyer. Impair the Timeshift Stone through the roof grind.

Out in the foyer, search for a fan on the divider with light gushing through it. With the Timeshift Stone impaired, you can shoot the Eye Switch through the halted fan edges.

This will open the southeastern entryway in the foyer. Enter it and move the square far removed on the close by stage. You would now be able to shoot an eye switch through this fan, however you should remain on a story change to open it.

Remain on the floor switch and line up your shot. This opens the last entryway in the lobby (the southwestern entryway). Presently, get back to the lobby and enter the northwestern entryway where you recently turned on the boat's motor. Hit the Timeshift Stone with your Bow through the mesh in the roof to turn it on.

Head once again into the southwestern entryway and kill the Technoblins in the room. You can enact the second, and last, motor switch here by wounding it with your sword.

Go to the foyer once more, enter the northeastern entryway and move out of the window by the raft. Bring the stepping stool down to B3.

Floor B3

In the motor room, the entirety of the cylinders ought to be moving. You should keep away from these via cautiously timing your runs.

A Whip hold can be found over a pit simply past the main arrangement of cylinders. You can utilize this to get to the Treasure Room. Utilize your Whip to get the hold and utilize A to quit swinging. Position yourself to confront the edge on the western side with a stepping stool and swing over to it.

Floor B1

This stepping stool prompts a room with 5 Chests in it, containing 3 uncommon Treasures and 2 Silver Rupees!

Floor B3

Head down the stepping stool to the motor room. The last stretch of cylinders is more earnestly to navigate. You can utilize the Whip grasp to swing onto the primary cylinder, yet you need to hang tight for it to rise, and the other to fall, to leap to the following.

On the far side, pull the divider change to make an alternate way. Slither in the little opening and you can ascend a stepping stool up to the extension on B2.

Floor B2

Free the robots and they will give you a Small Key. You can utilize this key on the deck of the boat to get to the Captain's Cabin. End the raft up to the deck.

Floor F1

Note that you can utilize your Whip to take the Bokoblins' Monster Horns now, in the event that you should stumble into a Bokoblin calling for reinforcement.

Hit the Timeshift Stone on deck to handicap it. Enter the locked entryway on deck with the Small Key and head down the steps.

In the Captain's Cabin you can save at the Bird Statue. In the open room you can shoot the Timeshift Stone through the mesh in the roof to enact the room's adversaries. Make certain to not to forfeit your Shield by allowing the Beamos to destroy it - a Shield Bash can send its bar back at it to paralyze it. On the other hand, you would now be able to utilize your Bow to shoot the Beamos' eye to kill it in a flash. With the adversaries far removed, remain on the red floor switch and shoot a bolt at the Eye Switch through the opening in the divider.

This will open the entryway into the following room. This room has three Beamos in it, so don't simply run in daze. Stay back and kill at their eyes with the Bow.

When all the Beamos are killed, the room with the last Chest will open. Inside is the Squid Carving (Boss Key).

Floor B2

The Boss Door is on B2. Head here and save prior to opening it. Sit on a stool by the Bird Statue to recuperate your full wellbeing prior to heading into the manager entryway.

Spot the Squid Carving in the Boss Door so the cutting looks like a skull with the red eye in the center confronting outward.

The arms that destroy the boat must be cut with a Skyward Strike. Charge your sword and release an upward cut to move them.

Advance up the steps, evading barrels and cutting appendages. When you get to the deck, the supervisor will uncover himself.

Tentalus

Tentalus is an enormous ocean beast with a solitary, clear flimsy part: it's gigantic eye. Shooting the eye with a bolt will continually cut the beast down so you can cut at its eye. The issue is having a spotless chance.

Toward the beginning of the battle you need to cut a couple of arms with your Skyward Strike capacity. To do this, hold the blade in an upward direction so it charges, then, at that point go around to try not to get hit. Lock on to a close by limb and release the sword's energy with a flat slice to slice the arm down the middle.

Do this to 3 or 4 limbs and the Tentalus will ascend, permitting you to hit its eye with a bolt. When the Tentalus tumbles to the deck, run up to its eye and slice it until it reels back for another round.

You need to rehash this cycle 2 additional occasions. Each time more limbs will blast through the deck so you need to charge your blade and release a strike rapidly. This is the place where moving around a ton and securing on comes convenient.

For the last period of the battle you should move onto the higher segment of the deck. Tentalus presently utilizes its arms on its head to assault - however these ones have close to nothing, freaky mouths. To have an unmistakable chance at its eye you basically need to cut at the arms quickly (a twist assault can help) until the monster stops its surge.

Shoot the eye and afterward run ready and cut at it with your blade. You'll need to rehash this whole cycle in some measure again to kill the monster.

Get your Heart Container and a cutscene will happen. After the cutscene, you will have a redesigned sword - with additional Dowsing spaces. Ultimately, Fi will start adding things like Gratitude Crystals to the potential Dowsing targets.

After you are gotten back to the dock, utilize the Bird Statue to get to the sky.

Note that you would now be able to play Rickety Coaster at the Shipyard for a Heart Piece assuming you need.

The Silent Realm - Eldin Volcano

Land at the Volcano Ascent Bird Statue. The Silent Realm entrance is here at the tone entryway. Take out your Goddess' Harp and play it to open the entrance. This time in the Silent Realm you can gather 15 of Din's Tears and 7 Dusk Relics. Obviously, you can generally re-play the level to load up on Dusk Relics.

Snap to develop map.

Here are probably the trickiest collectibles in The Silent Realm - Eldin Volcano:

You can take a steam vent only east of the beginning stage to the highest point of Eldin Volcano. There are three Tears in the slide locale of the space. One is not long before you bring the slide down.

Another is on a stage in the long slide. Take the correct way and focus on the arrival with the springs. Take these to the Tear.

Take the center way, then, at that point veer left to get the Tear on the actual slide.

One Dusk Relic is in a tree in the southeast region. Roll into the tree to cut it down.

Another Dusk Relic is stopped in the mass of the passage prompting the northeastern area from the beginning stage.

You can leap out to a rope, utilize the ANALOG STICK to re-position your swing and climb the rope somewhat, then, at that point swing into the Tear in mid air.

Crawl through the little passage in the southwest to discover a rope you can adjust on to arrive at a Tear

Save the northeastern region for last. Run up the right half of the slope keeping away from the foes totally by getting the Stamina Fruit and proceeding to the top. Here, snatch the Dusk Relic and Tear, and afterward slide down to the last Tear at the lower part of the eastern slide.

For finishing the Silent Realm you will get the Fireshield Earrings. These will keep you from consuming for quite a while when you burst into flames. Moreover, you would now be able to arrive at the Volcano Summit region!

Manufactured by Amazon.ca
Bolton, ON

21265010R00066